The Cruise
of the Arctic Star

The

Cruise

of the

Arctic Star

SCOTT O'DELL

Maps by Samuel Bryant

Beautiful Feet Books 2008

LIBRARY OF CONGRESS CONTROL NUMBER 2008925900

ISBN 978-1893103252

PRINTED IN THE UNITED STATES OF AMERICA

www.bfbooks.com

Cover: Photographs provided by Mrs. Elizabeth Hall. Used with permission of the
Scott O'Dell estate
Artistic Design: Rea Berg
Graphic Design and Layout: Shaun Ledgerwood,

Also by

SCOTT O'DELL

The Black Pearl

The Dark Canoe

Island of the Blue Dolphins

Journey to Jericho

The King's Fifth

Sing Down the Moon

The Treasure of Topo-El-Bampo

The Serpent Never Sleeps

Streams to the River, River to the Sea

The Cruise
of the Arctic Star

To the Navigator,
in all weathers and all the seas

Scott O'Dell
1898-1989

Scott O'Dell, winner of the Hans Christian Andersen award for his children's works, is most widely known for his Newbery Medal winner, *Island of the Blue Dolphins* (1960). This historical fiction is based upon the real life of Karana, an Indian girl who survives alone for 18 years on an island off the California coast. In recreating her story, O'Dell draws from his broad knowledge of California's wildlife, Indian customs and practices, and his deep respect for the beauty of the landscape of his native state. His portrait of Karana depicts a brave girl who survives by her own wits and resourcefulness, and readers identify with her struggles against wild dogs, loneliness, an earthquake, storms and the vagaries of living in the wild, building her home, hunting, fishing and preserving food for the winter months. This Robinsonade novel with a twist—since it really happened—is still a favorite of children today.

Three of O'Dell's other novels for young people— *The King's Fifth, The Black Pearl,* and *Sing Down the Moon* all received Newbery Honors, and his novel *The Hawk That Dare Not Hunt by Day* tells the dramatic life story of William Tyndale and the terrible price he paid to provide the first English translation of the Bible. Of O'Dell's many literary accomplishments, he is particularly regarded for the ways in which he depicted female protagonists that played key roles in history, but were seldom the subjects of books for young people. In this endeavor he wrote historical novels of both Sacajawea and Pocahontas—*Streams to the River, River to the Sea* and *The Serpent Never Sleeps* respectively. *Sing Down the Moon* features Bright Morning, a young Navaho girl whose tribe is forced into reservations on the Long Walk of 1864. Each of the above novels present richly crafted characters set against historically accurate panoramas that give history immediacy and meaning for young readers.

In *The Cruise of the Arctic Star*, O'Dell takes a voyage up the length of the California coast in his cedar-hulled offshore cruiser named *Arctic Star*. With his wife Elizabeth along as skilled navigator and cook, a friend Del as cohort and deckhand, and an unpredictable hired hand named Rodney Lambert, the crew journeys up the coast and experiences first hand the delights and drama of life at sea along this beautiful shoreline. Along the way, the author relates the colorful narratives of California's past through the stories of men and women like Cabrillo, Viscaino, Junipero Serra, Kate Sessions, Kit Carson, Jedediah Smith and many more. Drawing from journals of other notable visitors like Richard Henry Dana, Robert Louis Stevenson, and Sir Francis Drake, readers are given a window into life in California hundreds of years ago. O'Dell offers readers dramatic incidents seldom featured in text books on California history—like the worst peacetime disaster in the history of the United States Navy that occurred in the treacherous Jaws of the Devil near Point Conception. Readers will delight in the story of Jedediah Strong Smith's wrestling with a grizzly and the wilderness friend who stitched his ear and face back together—with no anesthesia, of course! Pirates have to play a part in a land so rich in coastline—and they do, with buried treasure on a Southern California isle known as Dead Man's Island. The stories of the discoverers, explorers and settlers of California have never been drawn so delightfully as they are under O'Dell's pen. With his love of his native state, his knowledge of the landscape, sea life, and historical past of this region, O'Dell's work continues to stand as an important contribution to the rich literature of the Golden State.

Rea Berg, 2008

Introduction

The Cruise of the Arctic Star is the story of a voyage from San Diego to the Columbia River, along the California and Oregon coasts. It's the first part of a longer voyage that took four summers and went on along the coast from the Columbia to Seattle, through the Inland Passage to Alaska.

Much of the story is a voyage into the past. It follows in the wake of the Spanish explorers Juan Cabrillo and Sebastian Vizcaíno, the English pirate Sir Francis Drake, the merchant sailor Richard Henry Dana and captains of the New England clippers. It also follows the footsteps of such landsmen as Father Serra, Jed Smith, Lean John, Kit Carson and John Sutter. So the book has to do with the land and the sea, the past and the present.

For those interested in boat details, *Arctic Star* is an off-shore cruiser, modeled after the Alaskan fishing trawlers, designed by Ed Monk and built in Seattle. She is fifty feet overall, displaces thirty-two tons and is planked with two-inch Alaskan cedar on steam-bent oak ribs. She has a General Motors diesel engine, an Onan generating plant, two banks of thirty-two-volt batteries — eight batteries to a bank. Her tanks hold one thousand gallons of fuel and nine hundred gallons of water. Her cruising range is about thirteen hundred miles.

For those interested in learning the simple rules of coastal navigation, it is well to remember that you can easily get lost in a boat and that it is up to the navigator to see that you don't. He must know the proper course to steer and at what time you'll arrive in port. This sounds simple, as if all he needs to do is look at the chart, draw a pencil line between where you are and where you want to go and sail away. But the task is more complicated than that. The pencil line is only the beginning.

First, the navigator uses his parallel rulers — two rulers fastened together so that they move back and forth but are always parallel to each other — and places one of the rulers on the pencil line, the other ruler through the exact center of the compass rose that appears on every chart. (The rose appears on all the charts in this book, too, though in simple form — a replica of the boat's compass, which is divided into 360 degrees.) The place where the line crosses the compass rose gives the navigator the boat's true course. Unfortunately, the navigator cannot steer by this course.

Because the earth's magnetic pole (toward which all compasses point) is different from the world's real North Pole, the navigator must now correct this true course by adding or subtracting the amount of variation caused by the magnetic pole. The chart shows exactly what this variation will be.

But the magnetic course is apt to be wrong. Boats have iron in their hulls and often are filled with magnetic equipment, such as depth finders, generating plants, radar and radio. The boat itself makes its compass deviate from the magnetic pole. And what is worse, it will deviate a different number of degrees when headed in different directions. These deviations are put down on a card and kept ready for use.

So that the navigator won't forget to make all the corrections, he may use a handy slogan: "Can Dead Men Vote Twice?" The question is a formula: C (compass course) + D (deviation) = M (magnetic course) + V (variation) = T (true course). The formula works both ways. When plotting a course, you work from the chart reading to the boat's compass. When finding out where you are, you work from the compass heading to the chart.

For example. Suppose that the true course the navigator has found — using parallel rulers and the compass rose — is 305°. Because he is beginning with the true course, he must work backward on his formula, "Can Dead Men Vote Twice?" He subtracts fifteen degrees from the true course, which gives him a magnetic course of 290°. But his compass deviates three degrees west in this direction — so he adds three degrees to the magnetic course and comes up with a compass course of 293°.

Once the boat is under way, the navigator uses dead reckoning to estimate his boat's position. By multiplying the speed of the boat by the hours traveled, the navigator knows how far along the course line his ship has sailed. But he must allow for both wind and ocean currents, since both water and wind can speed up a boat or slow it down.

The coasts and waterways of the United States are charted, and the charts may be purchased from the government or a marine supply store at a nominal cost.

A short list of books may be found at the back. I hope it

will encourage the more adventurous readers to explore for themselves things spoken of in the story — the weather, for instance, the trees of the Pacific Coast, the sea itself and the lives of the creatures that share this world with us.

The Author

ONE

The Greek God

1

Thursday. Clear and warm. Wind in the afternoon, 8-10 knots from the west-northwest.

So READS the weather report for San Diego, but the day
is not clear. It dawns with a heavy fog that hides the sun
and the harbor. It is a day when smart sailors turn over in
their bunks, take a look out the porthole, and go back to
sleep.

Rod Lambert shakes his head. He is leaning against the
exhaust pipe that runs from the engine room through the
galley and up to the flydeck. We are in the galley drinking
coffee.

"We better cool it for a couple of hours," he says. "Man,
it's sure thick."

I don't know why I am getting to dislike Rod Lambert.

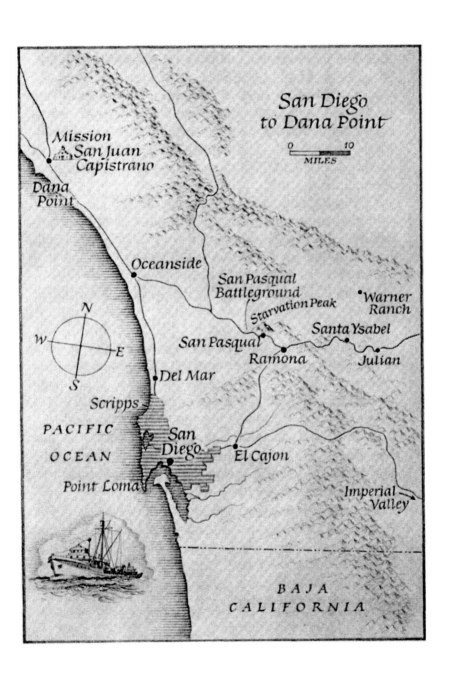

San Diego
to Dana Point

0   10
MILES

Mission
San Juan
Capistrano

Dana
Point

Oceanside

San Pasqual
Battleground

Starvation Peak

Warner
Ranch

San Pasqual

Santa Ysabel

Ramona

Julian

N

W   E

S

Del Mar

Scripps

PACIFIC

OCEAN

San
Diego

El Cajon

Point Loma

Imperial
Valley

BAJA
CALIFORNIA

Since I've only known him for three days, it seems foolish. What is it that I don't like? It worries me. Is it his mustache? Well, I have worn a mustache myself, less handsome than his. He has on a week-old shirt, grimy around the collar, but we are not going to Sunday School. We are headed north for the Columbia River and then on to Alaska — to Sitka and Taku and Skagway — through a lot of rough water.

"We've been trying to leave for three days," I say.

The reason we haven't left, I suspect, is that Rod Lambert has a girlfriend in port. We are to learn that he has girlfriends in every port on the Pacific coast.

"Captain, it's up to you," he says.

Maybe it's because he calls me "Captain" that I dislike him.

"Anything you say, Captain."

There it is again. This time it is in his best stage voice, a husky whisper, as if he were standing in front of a Technicolor camera, playing Steve McQueen. He has many voices, each to suit the moment, but this is not why I dislike him.

He still leans, hugging the big exhaust pipe with one arm. The engine has been running for ten minutes and the pipe is warm. Rod is a great cross-legged leaner. He sips his coffee and waits for me to speak.

He is about twenty-one and so tall that he has to stoop to clear the carlings overhead. He is wide in the shoulders and narrow in the hips, and has a crop of curly blond hair that fits like a helmet. His head is round and his features are perfect. He looks like one of those stone gods they dig up in Greece from time to time.

3

"The fog'll burn off when the sun shows," he says.

"Yesterday the sun didn't show until noon," I answer.

"It will show earlier today," he says. "It's a routine. Three days straight, everything's socked in. Then the fourth day it begins to clear early. The fifth day it dawns clear. Tomorrow is the fifth day. It's a regular routine, man."

He has the weather all figured out so he can spend another evening in San Diego. He pours himself a third cup of coffee and comes back and leans against the warm pipe and looks out at the fog. A ship's bell rings somewhere in the channel. From far off comes the moan of the Point Lorna horn.

The engine-room door opens and Del Boyce comes out. He climbs the ladder into the main cabin, bumping his head on the way.

"I bump it every time," he announces.

"Why?" Rod asks.

"Because I'm stupid," Del says.

"That's a good reason," Rod says. "My granddad used to bump his head all the time. We had a lamp that hung down over the dining-room table and every time he got   up from the table he would bump his head. We finally moved the table before he knocked all his brains out. It was hard to teach Granddad anything. We finally gave up trying."

They glance at each other and I pour Del a cup of coffee, feeling embarrassed because he is a friend and a guest. Del isn't as tall as Rod Lambert, but he is bigger and tougher. He can drive a spike with his fist. He can take care of himself. Yet, I feel embarrassed.

4

We are still tied up to the dock, but the bickering has started already. We have two thousand miles and more to go. I wonder if we'll make it.

"What do you think?" I ask Del.

"About what?"

Del is an experienced sailor.

"The fog," I say. "Shall we go or wait it out?"

"Go."

I walk over to the panel and flip the radar switch. From the flydeck comes the soft hum of the scanner turning. My wife appears from somewhere, looks out at the fog and says nothing. Whatever it is, wait or go or stand on your head, Elizabeth is for it, usually.

She goes out with Del to unfasten the lines, two lines forward and two aft. Del shouts that all is clear. I glance at the dial that gives the position of the rudder. It shows dead center and I press the reverse button and hold it down until the gear takes hold, and with a long warning blast on the air horn we back out of the slip and make a slow turn into the channel.

Quiet as a shadow a thin gray shape looms across our bow. It could be a hundred yards away or a hundred feet. The eye picks it up as a mist-shrouded coast. Or a tropical island fringed by palms. Or a piece of Antarctica washed by frozen seas. Our radar sees the shadow for what it is — the aircraft carrier *Bunker Hill*. She lies moored about two hundred yards ahead and I make a fast move to starboard, to the right.

Overhead the slow-turning scanner watches the harbor. What it finds it puts down with a ghostly pencil on a pale green screen the size of a sheet of paper, but round.

It puts down what it sees in exact detail, so that you are looking at everything that lies within a fifteen-mile circle. To see the image in sharper focus, there is a rubber hood that encloses the screen. It fits over your eyes as you peer down at it and blocks out all the light.

We are in the main channel, heading south. If we keep this heading we will miss *Bunker Hill* and pass safely between Point Lorna to starboard and Coronado Reef to port. But to the eye, looking out at the fog, we are lost. We are not even passengers on a small boat feeling its careful way. There is no sea beneath us and no sky above and no up or down and no port or starboard. There are no sounds except the hum of the scanner overhead and the throb of the big Diesel below.

I am at the wheel and my wife still watches the radar screen. I am ready to turn the wheel in any direction she tells me, to reverse the engine and stop. We are traveling at about three miles an hour.

"All clear," she says. "No boats approaching or overtaking."

Little Goat

2

Water runs down the window in front of me and I turn on the wipers. There is nothing to see. I think of Juan Rodriguez Cabrillo, who sailed into this same harbor in the year 1542. Juan was the first. He came from

Natividad on the west coast of Mexico in command of two small ships.

Ships is too grand a word for *La Vitoria* and the *San Salvador*. They were thrown together on the beach out of driftwood and scraps of timber and a handful of metal. They were high in the poop, almost as broad as they were long, top-heavy, and balanced like a yo-yo. Crablike, they often moved sidewise as fast as they moved forward. If you have seen pictures of Columbus' *Santa Maria*, then you will recognize them.

Yet Juan Cabrillo brought these two little caravels into the bay after fifteen hundred miles of uphill sailing, against wind and current and a dangerous coast. He sailed without charts because the coast had not been charted. Without an engine, of course. And without a radar.

"What do you see?" I ask the radar operator. "Nothing."

"It better be something."

"I see the Kona Kai Marina. The Coast Guard Station. Point Loma. The Navy submarine base. Four channel markers . . ."

She is being funny. I glance at the compass and go back to Juan Rodriguez Cabrillo. He was twenty-three years old when he brought his two ships into San Diego harbor. I have often wondered what he looked like. The pictures I have seen of him were obviously fakes. They are like the pictures police artists make of wanted fugitives, pictures that look like four or five different people, but no one especially.

Cabrillo means "little goat" in Spanish. So Juan might

have looked like a goat — long and elegant in the jaw, a tuft of rough hair sprouting low on his forehead, and a goat's wise, yellow eyes. He must have been small in the body. All of these Portuguese and Spanish conquistadores were small. We know this because of the clothes and armor they left behind. There was not a basketball player or linebacker in the lot. A height of five feet six inches would be a good guess for Juan Cabrillo.

"We are passing Ballast Point," my wife says.

When Cabrillo sailed into the harbor in 1542, Ballast Point was covered with stones twice the size of your fist that were all colors and tumbled smooth by the sea. A hundred and fifty years ago, captains returning to Salem and Boston with half-empty ships took tons of these stones along as ballast, and many of the New England streets are paved with them. Now it is just a name on the chart, difficult to find even when it is not hidden by fog.

Lambert and Boyce are on the flydeck. The intercom is open up there but not here in the cabin, so I can hear them but they can't hear me.

"What do you think of Lambert?" I ask my wife.

She stands bent over the radar screen, her face pressed down against the rubber shield. She is concentrating and doesn't hear me until I ask her again.

"He's all right," she says. "Why?"

"He bothers me."

"It's sort of late now that we're on our way. Remember that we scoured the waterfront trying to find someone."

She is right. We did scour the waterfront. We are

8

lucky, I guess, to have anyone, even Rodney Lambert.

From the flydeck, over the intercom, comes the voice of the young man we are talking about. Rod is arguing with Boyce over whether a round-bottom displacement hull is better than a flat-bottom planing hull.

"The planing hull is faster, twice as fast, and just as seaworthy," Rod says.

Del Boyce is a shipwright and has built everything from ten-foot skiffs to one-hundred-foot tuna clippers. He has three brothers who are shipwrights and the four of them have been building boats for twenty-five years.

"Faster but not as seaworthy," Del answers.

"I've been in both and I'll take a flat bottom any day. The trouble with you, Boyce, is that you build boats but you don't go anywhere in them. I've fished Baja the last two winters and made Alaska three times."

His three trips to Alaska are why I hired him. I hope he has been to Alaska even once.

Our boat, the *Arctic Star*, has a round-bottom, displacement hull. I say to my wife, "How does a kid get to know so much? Boyce was building boats when Rodney Lambert was in diapers."

To my surprise Rodney answers. I've forgotten to turn the right switch and my voice is coming through to him up there on the flydeck.

"Captain, you don't have to have a long gray beard," he says to me, "before you learn that a flat-bottom, planing hull is . . . "

I flip the switch and turn him off.

"Two of something dead ahead," Elizabeth says.

"How far? How big?"

"Very small and about a quarter of a mile. They could be rowboats."

We are going as slowly as we can at a speed of one and a half knots, so I press the neutral button and we coast and glide past the two objects that turn out to be brown pelicans floating on the water. This is a surprise, because most of the pelicans around here have been killed off.

The horn on Point Loma sounds at regular intervals. Elizabeth reports that Number One bell buoy lies straight ahead at a distance of a mile, and here the boat lifts and gently rolls to the first of the long Pacific swells. I turn the wheel and head NW on a reading of three hundred fifty - two degrees and open the throttle to 800 RPMs. Still feeling our way at half speed, I open the window to the right of the wheel, put my head out, and breathe the morning wind. The harbor smells have gone. The wind has the taste of kelp and the sea.

Once more I think of Juan Rodriguez Cabrillo and how he sailed up from Mexico along this coast, without radars or engines or charts. I admire this young man they called the "little goat." We will cross his wake again, farther north along the coast of California where he happened into stormy seas and eventually died.

Serpent on the Rock

3

Another of these young sailors I admire was Sebastian Vizcaíno. Not so modest nor so engaging as Cabrillo, he was familiar with the sea and a very inventive cartographer.

Great giver of names to California islands, harbors and headlands, Sebastian Vizcaíno came along in 1602, sixty years after Cabrillo sailed into San Diego Bay. Cabrillo named the bay San Miguel. Vizcaíno changed the name to San Diego de Alcalá. He called Ballast Point the Point of Pebbles. We shall meet him again a few leagues up the coast, still giving out names left and right.

The history of Spain in California was a series of bold and breathless leaps into the unknown. Spanish explorers would find something valuable and then, likely as not, it would be forgotten. After Vizcaíno explored the coast and named and renamed everything, California sat for one hundred and thirty-nine years as if it had never been discovered.

Then in 1741 things began to happen. Vitus Bering, a Dane sailing under the Russian flag, found the strait that bears his name, sailed along the Aleutian Islands, sighted the St. Elias Mountains in Alaska, and claimed everything that he saw for the czar.

The Spaniards grew uneasy. They held long talks about the Russian danger. But while they talked, the Russians backed up their discovery by building ships on Kodiak Island and sending them out to trade in the newfound lands.

For twenty-six years the Spaniards talked. Then the king got off a hurried letter to Mexico City, commanding the viceroy to put into effect a plan that had long been considered. The plan was simple. Missionaries would be sent into Baja California to man all the churches that were abandoned when the Jesuits were sent back to Spain. Other missionaries were to press on into Alta California — to San Diego, to Santa Barbara, and to Monterey. Each of the three missions, as it was built, would be protected from Indian attack by a garrison of soldiers.

The small band of missionaries was put in the charge of Junípero Serra.

Father Serra wore steel-rimmed spectacles and had a high, thin, Spanish forehead. He was a small man — five feet two inches — worn to the bone, and very lame.

When he traveled from Spain to Vera Cruz in Mexico, and was on his way to Mexico City, Father Serra refused to ride the horse that was offered him. He liked to walk and he walked everywhere he went. Like his idol, St. Francis, he needed to feel the earth under his feet.

It was more than a hundred miles to Mexico City, a long climb through jungle and across flooded streams, but Father Serra came near the end of his journey without mishap. He was walking in grass when of a sudden he felt a sharp sting on his leg. At first he thought it was the sting of a hornet, but looking back he saw a snake gliding away.

Brother Pedro, his companion, snatched up a stick and turned to kill the serpent that now lay coiled upon a rock. Though gripped by pain, Serra cried out, saying that he must not kill the serpent, it had meant him no harm. Brother Pedro obeyed his command and the two men pushed on to a village where the wound was dressed. In the morning Serra's leg was badly swollen. An open sore appeared, and in his lifetime it never healed.

Father Serra's forgiveness of the serpent was also in the spirit of St. Francis. It was St. Francis who, robbed of his tunic by a thief, ran after the thief to give him his sandals.

In Mexico City Father Serra became very popular. Hidalgos, their hats bedecked with diamonds, riding horses hung with gold and silver baubles, dismounted from their steeds and knelt in the streets to kiss his hand, feeling that they were touching a saint. Fashionable women flocked to the cathedral where he preached and sipped chocolate while, half in delight and half in fear, they watched him beat his breast with a stone and scourge his bare shoulders with a chain, in penance for their sins — for their sins, not his.

Once a poor laborer ran up the pulpit steps, took the chain from the father's hand, tore off his own shirt and shouting, "I am the sinner who should do penance," flogged himself so badly that he died of his wounds.

Junípero Serra could also be jolly, like Brother Juniper whose name he had taken when he joined the Franciscan order. Brother Juniper was the light-hearted companion of St. Francis, and Father Serra admired him and perhaps secretly wished to be like him. For twenty years Father Serra traveled the mountain trails of Mexico on foot with a small cross, and floated down tropical rivers by canoe and raft, preaching the gentle message of Jesus. "Amar a Dios," he said. "Love God."

For these reasons, he was chosen to lead the small band of missionaries into Upper California. But when the commander of the troops, Gaspar de Portolá, left the town of Loreto in Lower California, Father Serra was unable to walk or ride because of his leg. Portolá told him to choose someone else to take his place. Serra refused, rested for a few days, then asked to be put upon his mule, which trotted off to catch up with Portola and the soldiers.

Before Portolá left Loreto, two small packets, *San Carlos* and *San Antonio*, were sent north to San Diego. The ships were crammed with all manner of supplies — bread, flour, rice, beans, dried meat, corn, figs, dates, raisins, chocolate, brandy, smoked hams, six head of cattle, even a crate of chickens.

San Carlos met stormy seas and was blown far south to the vicinity of Panama. It took her one hundred and ten days to make the voyage from Loreto to San Diego. *San Antonio* arrived in half that time and was lying at anchor waiting when the San Carlos came into the bay. The captain of the *San Antonio* saluted the *San Carlos* but received no reply. Alarmed by the silence, he rowed out to her and was horrified to learn that she was a death ship. Ninety men — soldiers and artisans and sailors — had sailed with her from Loreto. Of that number almost sixty had died and had been buried at sea. Of those who survived, only five were able to stand.

Father Serra reached San Diego — at that time it was just a name given by Cabrillo to a beautiful bay — after traveling more than eight hundred miles through wild country. He had stopped only once while the blacksmith heated an iron and burned out the wound on his leg. Like Cabrillo and Vizcaíno we shall meet him again.

The Unsilent Sea

4

Playing tag with the sun, we run in and out of patches of dense fog. Off to starboard one of the kelp-cutters is at work. It is wandering along through a kelp bed like a cow browsing in a meadow. The cutters, which are as big as ferryboats, used to harvest all of the kelp and in this way robbed the fish of their homes. Now by law they can cut only part of the kelp and at certain times of the year. It is a valuable crop. It is used as an emulsifier, which acts as a thickener for salad dressing, beer, toothpaste, and ice cream.

We are passing the pier at La Jolla that belongs to the Scripps Institute of Oceanography, which stands on the bluff behind it. There is no wind and the sea is flat. Small waves are breaking on the beach but there is no sound on the sea around us, at least nothing that you can hear.

Most people think of the sea as being silent except for the sound of waves along the shore. But this is not true, the sea is a universe of sound. The pier that we now are passing, for instance, is the scene of a tumultuous underwater chorus.

You need a hydrophone to hear it, but every year, Scripps scientists report, starting in May and lasting through most of September, a croaker chorus begins about sunset and "increases gradually to a steady uproar of harsh froggy croaks, with a background of soft drumming. This continues unabated for two or three hours." The noise level is the same as an airplane motor heard from fifteen feet away.

Doug Diener, a graduate student at Scripps, when we were talking about this chorus, reminded me that croakers swim through the seas of the world by the millions. What tumult there must be beneath the waves from these operatic fish!

But croakers are not alone in the sea, by some trillion billion billion fish or more. Nor do they alone talk and make noises. There is the sea horse that swims upright and nods its head from side to side and makes a sound through its tubular snout like the snapping of a finger and thumb. There are the Korean catfish and the silver eel and the file fish and alewife and ocean pouts — all of whom make noises. There is the blue runner that makes a thumping noise. And the threadfish that rasps. Pilotfish and rudderfish and dollarfish and moonfish and angelfish and foolfish and minkfish all make sounds. As do the grubby and scup and porgy, mullet, sculpin, sea robin, sapo, and hake. The tautog grunts. Cunner bark. The mola mola grinds its teeth like a pig. Others chirp and sizzle, and chew and click and fry and crackle and pop.

Not to mention the sounds made by dolphins. Nor the strange and lovely sounds made by whales, which may be heard on a record called "Songs of the Humpback Whale."

Besides this underwater chorus there are the sounds made by waves from the far Aleutians, by earthquakes, rain, grinding glaciers, tumbling stones, and the whirr of propellers like our own. The sea is not silent as it often seems to be. It is alive — bursting with life.

The Silver Trees

5

There is sun on the far hills but on the cliffs at Torrey Pines only the dark tips of the trees show through the fog. Passing Torrey and its pines, I always think of Kate Sessions and her silver trees. I can't see them now but they are there in the fog, off to the southeast.

Kate was born in New England and graduated from the University of California and came to San Diego in 1892. Dark-eyed, pretty, in love with everything that grew, she opened a nursery and brought things that people had never seen before — the cork oak from Spain, white birches from New England, more than one hundred varieties of flowering acacia from Australia. She went to the southernmost tip of Baja California and brought back three small plants and a hatful of seeds of the fan palm, and from the seeds raised two hundred fifty trees.

She cleared the wilderness and planted it with trees. The trees are grown now and stand all over the city and in Balboa Park, one of the world's beautiful places.

When she was eighty years old and stooped from tending her plants, Kate still had her nursery. Once she showed me a small tree, a slip, really.

"It's a silver tree and it grows on the foggy coast of

South Africa," she said. "The sailors there, as they come into port and see its silver shimmer on the headlands, say, 'The old lady's got her washing out again.' Some day the sailors here can say that, too, when they come into port."

I can't see Kate's silver trees but it's nice to know that they are there.

The fog is lifting and we can see the beach at Del Mar. The beach was once a wide belt of white sand, running for two miles and more. It shows now as a thin gray strip broken by outcroppings of black rock where small waves tumble and break. The outcroppings of rock are the bare bones of the earth, stony ribs that protrude through the earth's skin. In ten years or sooner, scientists warn, the sea will have swallowed what little sand remains. Only the primordial rock will be left.

I used to think that the ocean manufactured its own sand by the endless churning of waves against the shore. But this is not the way of it. Sand comes from the streams and rivers that flow into the sea. Dams hold back flood waters, but they also hold back the sand that makes beaches and replenishes them.

TWO

Army of the West

1

WE ARE running along the coast about six miles out. Off to port is the dim outline of San Clemente Island and between us and the island are five warships, one of them an aircraft carrier. We pick up a warning on the ship-to-ship radio that target practice is going on around San Clemente and to stay out of the area. We are well out of the area but we move farther away by steering close to shore.

Fighter planes from the carrier are flying over us now, high and fast, leaving long ribbons of vapor behind them. Del Boyce and Rod are sitting on the forward hatch. I can't hear what he is saying, but Rod has his hands flat together, imitating a plane banking on a turn. He has a pilot's license and has flown three hundred and seventy-five hours, he says. He is also a racing motorcyclist. Earlier, when we were inching through the fog, he kept muttering to himself that we were going too slow.

Elizabeth is at the wheel so I climb the ladder to the flydeck, where I have a good view of everything. The warships are painted gray and are hard to see, the way the sun is slanting down. Planes are landing and taking off on the carrier, and then come two booms that shake the deck.

Off to starboard are the wooded hills of Rancho Santa Fe and beyond them, at a distance of thirty miles, stands Starvation Peak. Near its base is San Pasqual Valley, where the bloodiest battle of the Mexican War took place.

The war began in 1846. President Polk wanted California, which Mexico had seized from Spain. The president didn't care very much how he got it, whether he bought it with cash, wooed it away by revolution, or even won it by going to war. Ready for any of the three courses, he sent a secret agent with a secret letter to the United States consul in Monterey. The consul was instructed to do all within his power to support some of the rich and powerful Californians who wished to revolt against Mexico. This and other acts quickly led to a war between Mexico and the United States and to the Battle of San Pasqual.

The war in California was pretty much a comic opera, with soldiers marching up the hill and then marching down again. In a few months it was over, or so the Americans thought, and scout Kit Carson was sent on horseback to Washington to report the good news.

Meanwhile, General Kearney, in command of the

Army of the West, had captured Santa Fe in what is now the state of New Mexico. Leaving part of his army to hold the town, he set out with four hundred of his men for the Pacific coast to lend any help that might be needed.

The army traveled fast until they reached Socorro, New Mexico. There they ran into Kit Carson, who was riding hard toward Washington with his message to the president. General Kearney was surprised when he learned from Carson that the California war was over. He divided his force at once, sent two thirds of his men back to Santa Fe, since they would not be needed, and went on his way with only one hundred twenty soldiers.

Kit Carson trailed along. It was the last thing in the world he wanted to do. He had set his heart on seeing his Spanish wife in Taos and taking his first ride on a railroad train and shaking hands with President Polk. He went along because General Kearney commanded him to.

The skeleton Army of the West, after terrible hardships, forded the Colorado River on November 25 and headed northwest through the desert, over much of the country that has been reclaimed since by Imperial Valley. The men were in bad shape before the crossing of the Colorado and in worse shape when they rode down the scorched and desolate trail known as the Devil's Highroad.

Lieutenant William H. Emory, topographical engineer with the Army of the West, wrote in his diary:

"The sharp thorns were a great annoyance to our dismounted and wearied men, whose legs were bare . . . The day was intensely hot, and the sand deep; the animals, inflated with water and rushes, gave way by scores; and, although we advanced only sixteen miles, many did not arrive at camp until ten o'clock at night. It was a feast day for the wolves, which followed in packs close on our track, seizing our deserted brutes and making the air resound with their howls as they battled for the carcasses."

Leaving the desert for the first time in two months, the army reached Warner's Ranch. They spent a day in this beautiful valley, bathing in the hot sulfur springs and eating their fill — seven men finished off a whole sheep at a single meal. On half-dead mules and wild horses stolen nearby, they rode out of the valley on the morning of December 4. During the night word had come to General Kearney that a party of California lancers, the enemy, was camped not far away.

This is the Battle of San Pasqual that took place in the valley at the foot of the peak I am looking at now.

Surprise at Dawn

2

On that morning in December the sun rose in a murky sky and by the time the army was on its way to Santa Ysabel, rain was falling heavily. The men hunched in their saddles, many of them barefooted. They were a sorry-looking outfit. Only their eyes, sunk deep in their sockets, gave any hint that these Missouri farm boys were ready for battle.

General Kearney rode out in front of his bedraggled army on a gray horse that pricked up its ears at every sound. There were big brass rowels on his boots and he rode straight in the saddle as if it were not raining, his eyes fixed on the unknown hills that lay before him.

No one — neither General Kearney nor any of his officers, and scout Carson least of all — thought that the California lancers would stand and fight. Carson traveled up and down California and he had seen many of their Sunday soldiers. "They're a passel of old women," Kit Carson said.

General Kearney sent Lieutenant Hammond and fifteen men to locate the enemy. Hammond and his men came back to camp at two o'clock in the morning. He reported that they had stumbled upon some of the Californians sleeping in a hut at the foot of the canyon and by accident had managed to alarm them. General Kearney decided to march at once and the call "To horse! To horse!" was sounded. It was to be a surprise attack at dawn, and — using Indian tactics — an attempt to seize the enemy's horses.

Captain Johnson was listening to the mutter of saddle leather, his eyes on the twelve men in front of him, when he saw the distant shine of breakfast fires. The rain had stopped but the air was cold and thick with vapor.

General Kearney rode to the head of the column and with the first sign of dawn gave the command to break into a trot.

Captain Johnson spurred forward on his red gelding, taking scout Kit Carson with him. The twelve men followed and Lieutenants Warner and Emory and General

Kearney fell in behind them. Thus formed, the spearhead of the attack galloped down the brushy slope.

Through the mist Captain Johnson saw the California pickets, who were lounging beside their campfires, stagger to their feet and after a moment of confusion reach for their lances. Then they were running for their horses. They were in their saddles and fleeing in a wide circle down the valley and away from the charging troops.

Captain Johnson grasped the hilt of his sword; the braided rawhide was as hard as wood from the sun. Shouting to his men, he yanked on it, yanked again and again, and found to his dismay that the sword was rusted in its scabbard.

By now the fleeing Californians had regrouped. They wheeled their horses and brandished their lances, giving the fierce cry "Santiago!" — the rallying call of Spaniards since the days of the infidel Moors.

Captain Johnson drew his pistol from the holster and shouted again to his soldiers who were galloping up behind him. A musket was fired by one of the California horsemen. The ball struck Captain Johnson in the forehead.

Kit Carson had slipped his rifle from its case and as the musket shot struck Johnson, he aimed the rifle and pulled the trigger. He pressed the trigger a second time and a third time, and then realized that his powder was wet. Holding the rifle, he prepared to use it as a club.

The next instant his horse stumbled and Carson fell to the ground. He scrambled for his life beneath the on-plunging hooves of the advance guard. Crawling to one side, he sat dazed in the grass. Mist lay heavy around him. He saw the vague figures of the enemy riding in, with their lances raised. The lances were ten feet long or longer, made of river willows and tipped with iron files ground down to a sharp point.

General Kearney took a lance thrust in the shoulder and fell from the saddle. As he rose to his knees he took a second thrust. The lancer made a turn and was riding back to lance Kearney for the third time when a ball from Lieutenant Emory's pistol knocked him to the ground.

Only two musket shots had been fired by the Californians. One had hit Captain Johnson and a soldier had been badly wounded by the other.

Carson saw a rifle lying in the grass and ran for it. Again the powder turned out to be wet and would not fire, so he kept the rifle for a club and stared around him, his eyes groping through the mist.

The Californians had wheeled on their tough-muscled horses away from the advance guard and the men who lay sprawled on the ground. François Menard was dead. Captain Johnson was dead. The others, all except two of the twelve, were wounded. The advance guard of the Army of the West had been cut to pieces in three minutes of fighting.

Kit Carson heard the voice of Captain Ben Moore. The captain was at the top of a low hill on his big white horse, surveying the disaster spread out below him. After a moment he raised his hand and led the second wave of soldiers down into the valley.

The Californians were racing away on their strong horses toward the lower end of the valley. Standing in the high grass, holding the rifle that would not fire, Carson saw Captain Moore and Captain Gillespie sweep past, followed by shouting soldiers. They strung out in a long line, galloping toward the enemy that was now in retreat. Carson found a riderless horse and pounded down the trail to join the pursuit.

The Californians had ridden out of the valley and up a side trail through heavy brush. Carson could not see them any longer and he thought that they had escaped. Then they came out of the mist, a quarter of a mile to his right, and to the rear of Captain Moore's forces. Brandishing their lances, shouting "Santiago!" and moving with skill and speed, the best horsemen in the world, they again fell upon the Americans.

Captain Moore was down, lanced eight times. And Captain Gillespie, thrashing away with his sword, was down as well. More soldiers than Carson was able to count lay twisting in the grass.

The mist was clearing a little now, and Carson looked around for the foe. He thought he heard the sound of hooves climbing the hill to his right, but he was not sure and he saw nothing. The Californians had faded away like Indians.

Then Lieutenant Davidson came galloping in with his men, dragging two howitzers, but when the guns were being unlimbered the mules that were drawing one of them bolted and headed into the hills, though the driver sawed at their mouths. The howitzer clattered up a short rise and Carson saw a Californian come out of some thick brush and ride to meet it, holding a lance under his arm.

The lancer made a long thrust that caught the mule driver in the stomach and ran through him.

The sun was up somewhere in the east now. In the watery light the Army of the West gathered their forces. Taking their wounded, they slowly retreated to a steep hillside that was covered with cacti and loose rocks. From the first note of the bugle, not more than ten minutes had gone by, but in that time eighteen men had been killed and eighteen lanced. Of the lanced, two were to die that night.

The army spent most of the day gathering their wounded and carrying them to the hillside, though the Californians did not attack again. The rain and heavy clouds had drawn off, but the night came on bitter cold. Lieutenant Emory's reading showed two degrees below freezing.

Starvation Peak

3

With the coming of night Kit Carson got up a party and went out to gather the eighteen dead. The party dug graves as deep as they could with the tools they had and buried their men, putting rocks on the graves to keep the coyotes away.

The camp on the steep hillside, strewn thick with cacti and rocks, was cut off from water. All provisions had been lost during the battle, so there was nothing for the men to eat. Searching the hillside, they collected enough wood to make a small fire. Beside this fire Dr. Griffin, the army surgeon, tended the wounded.

The fires of the enemy showed brightly on a distant rise.

Toward midnight the camp began to settle down and the only sounds were the cries of the wounded and dying. Close after midnight Captain Turner, who had taken over command in place of the injured general, sent Alexis Godey and three other mountain men on a long detour to San Diego to seek help from Commodore Stockton.

Dawn broke slowly through an overcast sky. With the help of two men General Kearney was able to climb into the saddle. The army had been reduced by one third of its number, but he rallied them and they started off down the hillside, with their wounded stretched out on a sled made of two poles. On the skyline the enemy rode back and forth, but out of rifleshot.

The valley is flat here and in the winter a stream runs through it. What was left of the Army of the West traveled toward the sea and the harbor of San Diego. Two horses pulled the travois that held the wounded and soldiers rode on each side to protect them from attack. The horses and emaciated mules were watered at the stream and the men drank, lying in the grass. By chance they came upon a small herd of cattle, which they gathered up and drove before them.

When they reached the lower end of the valley a cloud of lancers beat down upon their rear, swept around them in a circle and occupied a peak that blocked their path. There was no other way the Americans could advance, so

General Kearney chose eight of his best riflemen to dislodge the enemy. Creeping forward through the brush while the rest of the army waited, they laid down a steady fire that finally drove the Californians off. The Americans moved up and camped, losing their cattle on the way.

At first they found no water on the peak, but some of the mountain men dug a hole and located a seepage, which was enough for the wounded.

Later that afternoon the enemy sent an emissary, under the protection of a white flag, with a gift of sugar and tea. When their emissary had gone, the enemy horsemen circled the hill, shouting taunts. That night three of the least emaciated of the mules were killed and the troops had their first meal in two days.

The next day dawned with white frost over everything. General Kearney had made plans to march that night but he found that the wounded were in no condition to move. The men ate what was left of the mule meat and throughout the day watched the lancers circle Starvation Peak, safely out of rifleshot. The enemy was waiting for them to surrender or die of thirst and hunger.

Toward night, since nothing had been heard from Stockton, General Kearney decided to send another party to San Diego. Lieutenant Beale, his Indian servant, and Kit Carson were chosen to go, scout Carson taking charge. San Diego was thirty miles away through rough country cut by steep arroyos and dense with cacti and chaparral.

Carson went slowly, Indian fashion, carefully picking his way. At dusk he had seen enemy sentinels at the base of the hill and he knew that the California camp was on the alert. He had no fear about himself. He had been in tight places before. He moved down the hillside with all the cunning learned during a lifetime spent on a dangerous frontier. His shoes ground on the rocks and made a noise, so he took them off and tucked them in his belt and told the others to do the same. Their canteens of water clinked as they went through the brush and they threw them away, keeping only their rifles.

An enemy patrol rode by and the three men hid behind a boulder, hid again at the sound of hooves, crawled on into a shallow ravine. Here the Indian left them to take another route, which Carson thought would increase the chances of someone getting through the circle of guards.

The two men crawled out of the ravine and Carson stood up to look over the ground that lay ahead of them. The next instant he sank in his tracks and was still. A sentry rode up to within thirty feet of them. Carson, pushing back softly with his foot, signaled Beale to hug the earth. The sentry slipped down from his saddle and put his ear to the ground and listened.

Then the horseman got to his feet, carefully brushed his knees, took out flint and steel, and lit a cigarette. The light flared over the rocks and the gaunt shapes of the prickly pear and the two men lying flat in the grass. Lieutenant Beale thought that this was a signal to the other horsemen who were patrolling the peak. He cupped his hand tight over Carson's ear and whispered, "Let's jump up and fight it out."

Carson did not answer at once. If the light was meant

for a signal, he thought, then the enemy has been alerted already and the best thing to do is to run for it, hoping that the darkness would conceal them. He heard no sound on the hillside, except the heavy breathing of the horse. He shook his head and put a hand on Lieutenant Beale to hold him back.

The sentry's cigarette went out and he lit it again and climbed on his horse. He wheeled around and started back along the way he had come, whistling softly to himself.

Carson and Lieutenant Beale began to crawl. The chaparral and cacti grew dense, and they had to get to their feet and walk. Around midnight, with the enemy patrols behind them, they stopped to dig the cactus spines out of their bleeding feet — somewhere along the way they had lost their shoes.

Back on Starvation Peak the night was bitterly cold, with the glitter of snow on the far mountains. Lieutenant Emory took a reading and announced that the temperature was four degrees below freezing. Near him lay young Streeter, with eight lance wounds in his head, five in his chest, and a wound in each hip. Dr. Griffin applied blisters to Sergeant Cox and bled him twice. Sergeant Cox, just a few months before, had married the prettiest girl in Fort Leavenworth. As morning dawned on the peak he died.

Around midmorning the enemy drove a band of wild horses up the hill in an effort to stampede the stock that was still left to the Americans. A sharpshooter killed three of the horses, which, being fat, were slaughtered and made into gravy soup.

During the day the Californians circled the peak, again out of range, and waited for the army to surrender. No one, least of all General Kearney, thought that Carson and his comrades would ever get through to Commodore Stockton. It was possible that they had been captured or killed already. And no one wanted to stay forted up on the peak, to die there of hunger and thirst.

At nightfall General Kearney ordered the baggage, saddles, and greatcoats burned — everything that could not be carried in a haversack. At dawn, on their half dead horses, they would try to cut their way through the enemy lines.

Bonfires blazed and went out and a smoky stench lay over Starvation Peak. Then around midnight the men heard the heavy tramp of boots on the hillside, the clink of canteens, and a voice calling up in the darkness.

One of the soldiers cried out, "Stockton! It's Stockton!"

It was not Stockton. But it was his men — one hundred seamen and eight marines. The siege was over. Next morning what remained of the Army of the West moved south to San Diego. Behind them they left those who had died in San Pasqual Valley and on Starvation Peak, the farm boys from Missouri who had fought in another needless war.

THREE

Swordfish!

1

WE HAVE SKIRTED the kelp and left the kelp-cutter astern. The coastline has a dent in it here and instead of following it we take a short cut and head for Dana Point.

A slight breeze has come up, the forerunner of the afternoon westerlies. Rod has fallen asleep over his magazine, but Del sits alert, holding the fishing rod in both hands. His line trails out astern, and far back, where the boat's wake makes a small platform before it levels out into smooth water, I can see the flying-fish bait leap and skip sidewise as it comes to the surface from time to time.

The best way to catch swordfish is with a long outrigger pole, which holds the line away from the boat. The line runs from the reel to the end of the outrigger and is held there by a clothespin. When the fish takes the bait and runs with it, before he decides whether or not he wants to swallow the bait, the tug of the running pulls the line from the clothespin and the line falls into the sea.

Del doesn't like this outrigger, though it catches more fish. It is better because the pause between the time the fish takes the bait and decides to swallow it is very important. If the fish feels any tension as he picks up the bait, he is apt to drop it. There is no tension on the line if it is hooked up on an outrigger and the line falls gently into the sea.

But Del doesn't like this system. He likes to sit with the rod in both hands and the line trailing straight out astern. He will sit for an hour this way, not moving, not even putting the pole in the holder in front of him. That may be the reason he has never caught a swordfish.

I don't see the fish take the bait. The first thing I see is Rod swing off the cabin top and lope along toward the stern and Del on his feet shaking the pole. I flick on the Intercom.

"Strike," I shout to the navigator.

The boat slows and stops dead in the water as the reverse gear takes hold, then coasts as we swing into neutral.

"What is it?" Rod asks.

"I don't know," Del says. "It don't feel like much."

"Let me feel," Rod says, taking the pole. He raises the tip slowly and waits, lowers it and waits. After a moment or two he hands the rod back to Del Boyce and says, "Hit him hard, man."

Boyce comes up on the rod.

"Hard. Not a love tap. Hit him hard," Rod yells.

The second time Del comes up hard on the rod, using all the strength of his arms, the rod bends nearly double and the reel whizzes and sings. The line changes its angle in the water, slicing toward the stern of the boat; then as I motion the helmsman to move forward a little, fearing that the line might get fouled up in the propeller, it points straight down.

"He's sounding," Rod says.

"What do you think it is?" Del asks.

"There are a lot of sharks in here," I break in. "Shovel nose and leopards."

"Have you ever caught a swordfish?" Rod asks.

"No," Del says.

"Well, you're catching one now," Rod says. "And you better sit down and take it easy, man."

Del, who is standing with his feet spread apart and the butt of the rod against his stomach, doesn't move.

Rod reaches in the locker, brings out a shoulder harness.

"I don't like those things," Del says, edging away.

"You'll like it in an hour or so," Rod says. "Maybe before."

"How big do you think the fish is?" Del asks.

"Two hundred. Give or take ten pounds."

The line is rasping off the reel and through the roller guides and the rod bends nearly double again, jerking as if a bucking burro were fastened to the other end.

"What size line you using?" Rod asks.

"Twenty-pound test nylon with a monel leader and a number-two hook," Del says.

"How much line?" "Three hundred yards."

"You're short-rigged," Rod says. "You haven't got

35

enough line. You should have more line and a bigger hook. The only thing you got right is the leader."

"I've got what I got."

"You're rigged up for yellowtail, not swordfish."

The fish is still sounding. Nothing has changed, except that we are drifting toward shore, which is about two miles away, near enough for us to hear the sound of the breakers, except that the reel is now a third empty.

"How deep is it around here?" Rod wants to know, looking down into water that is the color of woodsmoke.

"There are some deep spots," I answer. "About three hundred feet in places."

"If that's true, then he'll have to stop going down."

As if the fish were listening to our words, the position of the line changes instantly from straight down to an angle of forty-five degrees.

Rod looks over Del's shoulder at the reel and the drag. The angle has changed but the line is still running out.

"You better tighten up. We're going out too fast, man."

"Where do you get that 'we' stuff?" Del says. "Who's catching this fish, you or me?"

Nevertheless he tightens the star-shaped drag and the line, which has been taut, stiffens like piano wire and gives off a sound that seems a full note higher than it was before.

"Not so much. Loosen her a quarter turn," Rod says.

I wonder how long this two-handed fishing will go on. It will be a good thing if Del doesn't blow up, because he has never caught a big fish, at least one this big, and he needs the advice. Perhaps he would rather lose the fish than be told what to do. It irks me, this kind of fishing advice, so I wouldn't blame him.

Del doesn't hear this last instruction, or pretends not to, and the line continues to sing. Where it comes out of the water is well off on our forward quarter, so I motion Elizabeth to pull ahead slowly.

Her voice comes back on the intercom, "There's a lobster boat crossing our bow."

We drift until the lobsterman goes by. He is traveling fast, using a big Merc that pushes him along at about 20 knots, with traps piled in the stern and his storage box full of lobsters. I would hail him and buy a couple if we were not tied up to the fish.

Shark?

2

We haven't eaten since early morning and it is now about two o'clock. I drag out a bundle of sandwiches made that morning — it is always easier to prepare something before you leave the dock than it is to cook at sea, even a sea as calm as this one — and pass them around to the helmsman and the two fishermen. Del says that he is too busy to eat and I put his sandwiches away in the shade.

Rod says, "I'll take the pole if you want to eat."

Del pretends not to hear him. He asks for a drink of water and I suggest a Coke, but he wants water, which I bring in a pitcher. He drinks half the water, about a quart, and, holding the rod in one hand, pours the rest over his bald head.

The reel is half-filled now and still unwinding. Del has not tried to stop the fish yet. He is enjoying himself, but he is getting very short on line even though the drag is working. As long as the fish is on the line, he seems to be content to let him run.

"When are you going to start reeling?" Rod asks. "He'll keep running until you lay the pole on him."

After a moment Del comes out of his trance. Loosening the drag and putting his left thumb on the flat of the spooled line, he slowly lifts the rod, then quickly lowers it. As he lowers the rod he reels in the line he has stolen from the fish, which is two feet at most, and starts over again, up and down, lifting and lowering, pumping out of the sea and onto the reel a precious piece of line, two feet of it at a time.

"He must weigh more than two hundred," Del says, in no way discouraged.

"If he weighed more than two hundred," Rod replies, "he would be long gone. They don't come bigger than two hundred around here. Small stuff, man. Peru is where they come big. I caught one off Bahia that took sixteen hours to land. Started at seven in the morning and gaffed him at eleven by lantern light."

"How big?" I ask.

"One thousand thirty-seven pounds."

"That must be a world's record," I say.

"It would have been, man, if I could have weighed it when I caught it. But we ran into a storm and by the time we hit port, three days later, the fish had shrunk by forty pounds. Forty, at least."

"Sixteen hours is a long time to hang on to a pole," Del mutters.

"The longest fight on record," Rod says, "was thirty-two hours and five minutes. That was a black marlin off New Zealand, estimated to be better than twenty feet long. It towed a twelve-foot launch for fifty miles before it broke the line."

Del's fish is bucking like a burro again. Then he starts running out to sea. I ask the helmsman to move off to port a little and come around in a wide curve, which gives Del a chance to get back some of the line he lost in the last rush.

I fill a bucket with fresh water, pour some of it on the reel, which is too small for swordfish and is running so hot you can smell burning oil, and offer the rest to Del. He motions me to pour it over his head and I do. I watch him, hoping that he is not discouraged by Rod's Peruvian fish story. He does not seem to be, as he starts pumping again, two feet of line at a time.

He has been hooked on to the fish now for more than an hour and a half. He is red in the face but still strong. He stands with his feet braced against the lockers on either side of the stern. It would be better if he would slip on the shoulder harness with the straps that fasten to the rod so he would have the strength of his back, and not just his arms, when he pumps. Even the belt with a leather socket for the butt of the rod would help. He still has the rod stuck into his stomach. His stomach will be sore tomorrow.

The afternoon wind is coming up and we have a chop building. The line has been easy to see, slanting down into the quiet water, but the color of the sea has changed and the only way I can follow the direction of the line is to watch the tip of the rod. I am trying to help Del by shifting the direction of the boat. It appears to help some, for he has gained more than half of the line back.

"I wonder why he hasn't jumped," Del says.

"It could be a tuna," Rod suggests.

"I thought you said it was a swordfish," Del says.

"I still think swordfish. The trouble is, with that Mickey Mouse outfit, it's hard to judge what's happening or who's down there. It could be a leopard shark. If you let me take the rod I can tell better."

A short time after he spoke, the fish came up out of the water, straight up, up twice his length, dragging part of the sea with him, shaking his sword and his whole body. He was closer to the boat than I had thought. When he fell back into the sea it was hard to tell where he was because of the chop.

"I wasn't far off," Rod says. "One hundred and ninety or thereabouts."

Del is reeling in fast, taking in all the line the fish had lost in his leap. The fish makes one more run and as the boat swings her stern to the wind he shows about fifty feet out, near the surface and barely swimming.

Rod gets the gaff off the top of the cabin and, opening the gate in the stern, steps down onto the wide swimstep, holding on to the rail with one hand, ready to use the gaff with the other. He is left-handed, which makes it awkward, the way the boat and the fish are coming together.

"Bring him slowly," Rod says, "and to starboard. If he runs let him go. Steady. Keep your rod high and don't give him any slack. Keep the pressure on, man. A little more and I'll have him."

Holding the rail with his right hand, Rod bends down and reaches for the steel leader, using the gaff to bring the wire close enough to grab.

At this point I don't know what happened exactly. Maybe Rod didn't catch the leader with the gaff. Maybe he caught it and the leader slipped away as the fish turned broadside to the boat. All I really see is the fish looking up, his head turned so that only one of his eyes shows, like a small gold disk, looking at me and Del and then at Rod reaching for the wire leader.

As it turns out, Rod misses the leader, gives up trying to get hold of it and goes for the gaff. The fish is moving slowly toward the boat. The flat of the gaff but not the sharp point strikes him on the back. The force of the blow breaks the line away from the wire leader where they were held together with a swivel and the swordfish, as if he had been sleeping before, comes to life and drifts away.

Rod watches him disappear and says, "Sorry about that. But I didn't know you were going to let him turn."

"I didn't mean to let him turn," Del says. "But on the other hand, you're not much of a man with the gaff."

"We couldn't eat the fish if you had caught him," I say, trying to smooth things over. "All the swordfish around here are full of mercury poison."

"Not fit for human consumption," Rod says. "If you can't eat them, there's no point in catching them."

"The point is I would like to catch a swordfish," Del says.

"You will, you will," Rod says cheerily. "Just keep at it, man."

"Better luck next time," I say lamely.

The wind picks up and the chop turns into waves. We have lost a couple of hours during Del's adventure with the swordfish, so we put in at Oceanside instead of going on up the coast to Dana Point as we had planned.

Ship's Log

3

June 2: Oceanside has two jetties running out from the shore, parallel to each other and facing west. On a calm day with a light swell the harbor offers no problems, but in other weather care should be taken when entering or leaving. Coming in yesterday we did some sliding around on the breakers, which can be dangerous if there are other boats nearby. This morning the entrance is calm as we move out . . . about a mile on our way the navigator sights a whale spout. It is some two miles off our port bow and very faint. She thinks it is Gigi. She changes course and heads for the spot where we saw the spout. Meanwhile I turn on the radio in the hope of picking up a signal.

Gigi is the young gray whale that was let loose from Sea World three months ago. She weighed four thousand pounds when they captured her and put her on display at

Sea World. But she doubled in weight and was eating about a thousand pounds of squid a day so they got rid of her by putting her in the sea off the Scripps pier, where we were yesterday. She is equipped with a small sending radio fastened to her back and her back is painted with a large white mark. For a month she hung around the pier, not knowing what to do, and a lot of people criticized Sea World for turning her loose. They said she would die from loneliness or starvation, since she had been raised by hand in a pool, taught to do tricks, and knew nothing about the sea or other whales. But Gigi survived and after a few weeks worked her way north along the coast.

There is another spout a little south of where we saw the last one, but I can't pick up any signals on our radio. Then there are two spouts, thin fountains that catch the sun, close on our starboard bow, not more than two hundred yards away. Through the glasses I have a good look at both of the whales. They are yearlings, probably born in the early spring five hundred miles south of here at Scammons Lagoon. Their mothers have already gone north to their homes in Alaskan seas and will not come back until some other year, when they will have calves again at Scammons Lagoon.

There are two groups of whales. One group is called Odontoceti — "whales with teeth." The other group is called Mysticeti — "whales with mustaches." This last group is divided into three families: the fin whales, the right whales, and the gray whales — like Gigi. These whales have whalebone mustaches that hang from the roof of the mouth. When it is hungry, which is most of the time, the whale takes an enormous gulp of seawater, closes its jaws, and presses its tongue against the blades of the fibrous mustache. Thus the seawater is forced out through the blades, leaving behind in the whale's mouth whatever was in the water — sardines, anchovies, or other crustaceans.

Whales have been hunted close to extinction, like sea otter and polar bear. Last year the whaling fleets, mostly Russian and Japanese, killed forty-one thousand of these great mammals. In the old days men in wooden skiffs risked their lives to kill whales with harpoons in hand-to-hand conflict. Now the hunters cruise around in fast iron ships equipped with sonar, slaughtering them with high-powered cannon that fire explosive shells.

Either way — by hand or by cannon — whales have died by the millions. This is a description of the death of two whales, from a book by Frank Bullen, *The Cruise of the Cachalot*:

"Before it was fairly light we lowered, and paddled as swiftly as possible to the bay where we had last seen the spout overnight . . . The light grew rapidly better, and we strained our eyes in every direction . . . There was a ripple just audible, and away glided the mate's boat right for the near shore . . .

"Following him with our eyes, we almost immediately beheld a pale, shadowy column of white, shimmering against the dark mass of the cliff not more than a quarter of a mile away. Dipping our paddles with the utmost care, we made after the chief, almost holding our breath. His harpooner rose, darted once, twice, then gave a yell of triumph that rang reechoing all around . . .

"But, for all the notice taken by the whale, she might never have been touched. Close nestled to her side was a youngling of not more, certainly, than five days old, which sent up its baby-spout now and then about two feet into the air. One long, wing-like fin embraced its small body, holding it close to the massive breast of the tender mother, whose only care seemed to be to protect her young, utterly regardless of her own pain and danger . . .

"The calf continually sought to escape from the enfolding fin, making all sorts of puny struggles in the attempt. The mother scarcely moved from her position, although streaming with blood from a score of wounds. Once indeed, as a deep-searching thrust entered her vitals, she raised her massy flukes high in the air with an apparently involuntary movement of agony; but even in that dire throe she remembered the possible danger to her young and laid the tremendous weapon as softly down on the water as if it were a feather . . .

"So in the most perfect quiet, with scarcely a writhe, nor any sign of flurry, she died, holding the calf to her side . . ."

Ship's Log Continued

4

June 2: We sight three more yearling whales, but none of them turns out to be Gigi. They are moving northward at about our speed, sending up their shimmering plumes . . . There is a beautiful stretch of beach along here and a white surf and yellow, crumbling cliffs. In the days of the Spaniards, when there was scanty rain and little feed for the cattle, the rancheros, to save what feed there was, got rid of thousands of wild horses by driving them over these yellow cliffs . . . The beautiful shore belongs to the United States and the marines use it for landing drills and target practice. The government should let the public use it sometimes — on Saturdays and Sundays or during the hot summers . . . We pass the nuclear power plant at San Onofre, which sits on the cliff like a giant gumdrop. Part of the plant is open to visitors and there are tours and exhibits and lectures on how atomic power is created. Once I heard one of these lectures and didn't understand it. Perhaps I didn't understand it for the same reason that I don't understand what is wrong with the power output on our alternator or what makes the quacking sound in the bilge . . . We loaf along, enjoying the beautiful white surf and beach and the bare cliffs. It gives Del a good chance to catch a swordfish, but the best he can do is three small bonita. Rod keeps an eye on the fishing but saves his advice for himself. I think he has decided that Del is no one to fool around with. He hasn't decided about me yet. At six bells Dana Point looms off our starboard bow . . .

FOUR

Duck in the Bilge?

1

COASTING ALONG on the quiet shore of the Pacific [in the year 1834]," wrote Richard Henry Dana, Jr., "we came to anchor in twenty fathoms water, almost out at sea, as it were, and directly abreast of a steep hill which overhung the water, and was twice as high as our royal-mast-head. We had heard much of this place from the *Lagoda's* crew, who said it was the worst place in California. The shore is rocky and directly exposed to the south-east, so that vessels are obliged to slip and run for their lives on the first sign of a gale."

This is the description of Dana Point by the man it is named after. The steep hill he speaks about is still there, and it is still twice as high as a royal masthead. But the shore is no longer exposed to the southeast and vessels need not run for their lives at the first sign of a wind. It is now a snug harbor, protected by the granite arm of a breakwater. The harbor would please seaman Dana, especially if a gale were in the offing.

We arrive there in midafternoon and anchor in the channel, on a mud bottom that holds the anchor the first time it goes down. The shadow of Dana headland lies over the harbor and the headland cuts off the wind that has searched us out most of the afternoon.

We are no sooner at anchor than Del has his fishing rod in hand, the same one he used on the swordfish, and is clambering over the rocks on his way to fish the windward side of the breakwater. He has a pocketful of small hooks and anchovies and clams for bait, and has promised us fish for supper.

Rod and I go below to look at the filters that clean the oil before it goes into the engine. They are fitted with dials that tell you when they need to be changed. After a boat has sat at a dock for a month or so, sludge settles in the bottom of the fuel tanks. As soon as the boat goes to sea the sludge gets stirred up and, unless it is filtered out, the engine runs poorly or stops.

The filters are in good shape and we come to the regulator which controls the amount of electricity that goes into the batteries and works the same as a regulator in an automobile. I glance at it and pass on, though it is giving us trouble. To be more accurate, it has been giving all the marine mechanics in San Diego trouble. Marine mechanics have a lot in common with auto mechanics.

Yet another problem for this mechanic to solve is the shower. After you have carefully regulated the hot and cold water and have a comfortable mixture, suddenly the hot water shuts off and the cold water stays on. If you can stand this for exactly thirty-two seconds without freezing, you are in good shape. For in thirty-two seconds the hot water comes on again.

And maybe this mechanic, after he has solved the problem of the regulator and the water system, will be able to tell us what causes the quacking in the bilge.

The first time I heard the sound we were on Lake Union in Seattle and had just bought the boat. It was at dawn and I woke up hearing a noise that I thought was a duck swimming around outside. There are a lot of ducks on Lake Union that swim around looking for food. But when we left Lake Union and were headed down the coast for California, I heard the sound again.

I have heard the sound many times since and the mechanics have heard it too, but no one can find the reason for the quacking. It is possible that one of the Lake Union ducks somehow scrambled aboard and is hiding somewhere on the boat. But a good mechanic should be able to tell us if we have a duck, and, if we do not have a duck, then what can be done about the quacking.

Del Boyce could do something about all this if only he liked machinery. With hammer and saw and chisel he can build a fifty-foot hull as fine as any that ever went to sea. If you were shipwrecked on a tropical isle and wanted to leave, he could build you a boat out of driftwood and coconut shells. But even if Del liked mechanical things — things that slide and slither or make noises or go around and around in a circle — we still would have problems.

The truth is, a boat — any boat that travels the sea or just sits idly at the dock — lives in bad surroundings. Sun and wind and rain, salt and heat and cold, rust and electrolysis, barnacles, toredo worms, a dozen different kinds of pests, and the very sea itself all conspire to do it in. The enemy attacks methodically, timber by timber, bolt by bolt, nail by nail, parts above water and parts below water. The battle goes on night and day and never ends, not for the life of the boat.

Pondering the problems of the engine room, I remember the flydeck.

"Would you like to do some varnishing?" I ask Rod.

"No" he replies.

"Will you do some varnishing?" I ask.

"Yes," he says with his flashing white-toothed smile, "if you insist."

I send him off to the flydeck with a sheaf of sandpaper and instructions to sand everything in sight, which should take him two hours. Tomorrow we will varnish and lay up to let it dry. There is nothing like varnish in the fight against sun and salt air, nothing except good marine paint.

With Richard Henry Dana's *Two Years before the Mast* I crawl into my bunk, feeling a little guilty that I am not topside helping Rod. I have read Dana's book three times, first when I was fifteen. I have always liked it and read it each time with more pleasure than before, which for me is the test of a good book.

Traffic in Hides

2

Richard Henry Dana, Jr., was born in Massachusetts in

1815, not far from Harvard College. When he was sixteen he became a student at Harvard.

Dana ranked high in his studies, but before his freshman year was over he was suspended for taking part in a student rebellion and given six months in which to mend his ways. Two years later he caught the measles, and was left with eyesight so poor that he had to drop out of college.

Bored and with nothing to do, Dana decided to make a long sea voyage. He could have signed on as a supercargo, as a clerk. Instead, he chose the much harder life of a common seaman and joined the crew of the brig *Pilgrim*, bound out of Boston on a trading voyage to the California coast.

Dana spent two years on this adventurous cruise. When he got home he was a senior at Harvard and graduated at the head of his class in 1837. He went on to law school and three years later was admitted to the bar. It was during this time, while he was a student at Harvard and at law school, that Dana wrote *Two Years before the Mast*.

Dana's ship visited the headland where we are now anchored in order to pick up a cargo of tallow and cow hides. Mission San Juan Capistrano is located about two miles inland and at the time of the ship's visit was a flourishing center for cattle. Once the cattle had been slaughtered, the tallow and green hides were hauled to the headland and traded for goods the sailing ships brought from New England.

Dana describes his first visit to this place in the trading brig *Pilgrim*.

"Here the country stretched out for miles . . . and the only habitation in sight was the small white mission of San Juan Capistrano . . . We found several piles of hides, and Indians sitting around them. One or two other carts were coming slowly on from the mission, and the captain told us to begin and throw the hides down. This, then, was the way they were to be got down: thrown down, one at a time, a distance of four hundred feet!

" . . . Down this height we pitched the hides, throwing them as far out into the air as we could; and as they were all large, stiff and doubled like the cover of a book, the wind took them, and they swayed and eddied about, plunging and rising in the air, like a kite when it has broken its string.

" . . . As it was now low tide, there was no danger of them falling into the water, and as fast as they came to ground, the men below picked them up, and taking them on their heads, walked off with them to the boat."

The hard work came later. The hides had to be cleaned and salted, stretched and dried and carefully stowed in the ship, or else they would rot on the long, five-thousand-mile voyage around the Horn. The curing process was carried out at San Diego because of the good climate and because it was the last stop between California and home.

Dana did his share of work around the curing yards. His first visit to San Diego was typical of the several times he was there and of the way the work was done:

"When the hide is taken from the bullock, holes are cut round it, near the edge, by which it is staked out to dry. In this manner it dries without shrinking. After they are thus dried in the sun, they are received by the vessels, and brought down to the depot . . .

"Then begins the hide-curer's duty. The first thing is to put them in soak. This is done by carrying them down at low tide, and making them fast, in small piles, by ropes, and letting the tide come up and cover them . . .

"There they lie forty-eight hours, when they are taken out, and rolled up, in wheelbarrows, and thrown into the vats. These vats contain brine, made very strong; being sea-water, with great quantities of salt thrown in. This pickles the hides, and in this they lie forty-eight hours; the use of the sea-water, into which they are first put, being merely to soften and clean them. From these vats, they are taken, and lie on a platform twenty-four hours, and then are spread upon the ground, and carefully stretched and staked out, so that they may dry smooth.

"After they were staked, and while yet wet and soft, we used to go upon them with our knives, and carefully cut off all the bad parts . . .

"This was the most difficult part of our duty; as it required much skill to take everything necessary off and not to cut or injure the hide. It was also a long process, as six of us had to clean an hundred and fifty . . .

"This cleaning must be got through with before noon; for by that time they are too dry. After the sun has been upon them a few hours, they are carefully gone over with scrapers, to get off all the grease which the sun brings out. This being done, the stakes are pulled up, and the hides carefully doubled, with the hair side out, and left to dry.

About the middle of the afternoon they are turned upon the other side, and at sundown piled up and covered over. The next day they are spread out and opened again, and at night, if fully dry, are thrown upon a long, horizontal pole, five at a time, and beat with flails. This takes all the dust from them. Then, being salted, scraped, cleaned, dried, and beaten, they are stowed away in the house.

"Here ends their history, except that they are taken out again when the vessel is ready to go home, beaten, stowed away on board, carried to Boston, tanned, made into shoes and other articles for which leather is used; and many of them, very probably, in the end, brought back again to California in the shape of shoes, and worn out in pursuit of other bullocks, or in the curing of other hides."

A Good Dinner

3

There are a number of boats in the little harbor and a lot of calling back and forth, but I have no trouble hearing Rod at work on the flydeck, just over my head. He sands a strip of combing, then stops to light a cigarette (he has a lighter that you can light in a hurricane, with a lid that snaps shut with a bang). Then he says something to a girl on a boat moored nearby, laughs, goes back to sanding, but not for long.

Somewhere in *Two Years before the Mast* there is a description of a crew at work on Dana's ship. I have forgotten just where the passage is but keep looking until I find it. Half-listening to what is going on above, I read and ponder, more and more aware as I ponder that I lack the stuff from which captains are made:

"Anchor watch was kept all night, and at daybreak, 'All hands ahoy!' was called at the fore-scuttle and down the hatchways. Three minutes and a half were allowed for every man to dress and come on deck, and if any were longer than that, they were sure to be overhauled by the mate, who was always on deck, and making himself heard all over the ship.

"The head-pump was then rigged, and the decks washed down by the second and third mates; the chief mate walking the quarter-deck and keeping a general supervision, but not deigning to touch a bucket or a brush. Inside and out, fore and aft, upper deck and between decks, steerage and forecastle, rail, bulwarks, and waterways, were washed, scrubbed and scraped with brooms and canvass, and the decks were wet and sanded all over, and then holystoned.

"The holystone is a large, soft stone, smooth on the bottom, with long ropes attached to each end, by which the crew keep it sliding fore and aft, over the wet, sanded decks. Smaller hand-stones, which the sailors call 'prayer-books,' are used to scrub in among the crevices and narrow places, where the large holystone will not go. An hour or two, we were kept at this work, when the head-pump was manned, and all the sand washed off the decks and sides.

"Then came swabs and quilgees; and after the decks were dry, each one went to his particular morning job. There were five boats belonging to the ship — launch,

pinnace, jolly-boat, larboard quarter-boat, and gig, —
each of which had a coxswain, who had charge of it, and
was answerable for the order and cleanness of it.

"The rest of the cleaning was divided among the crew;
one having the brass and composition work about the cap-
stan; another the bell, which was of brass, and kept as
bright as a gilt button; a third, the harness-casks; another,
the manrope stanchions; others, the steps of the forecastle
and hatchways, which were hauled up and holystoned.

"Each of these jobs must be finished before breakfast;
and, in the mean time, the rest of the crew filled the scuttle-
butt, and the cook scraped his kids (wooden tubs out of
which the sailors eat) and polished the hoops, and placed
them before the galley, to await inspection."

It might be a good idea if I were to loan Rod this book
and urge him to read it. I might even underscore the passage I have just read and say something about how sailors
worked in the old days compared to how they work now.
But this seems sort of roundabout. Or I could just go up
and ask him how his new romance with the girl in the boat
next door is progressing. I do neither, being somewhat of a
mouse.

They are still talking back and forth as the ship's clock
strikes two bells, marking the hour of five. Bells to tell the
hour is a good system. If you hear three bells you know it
is half-past five, four bells six o'clock, six bells seven, and
eight bells eight o'clock. Then you start over again with
one bell. This takes for granted that you know within four
hours what hour of the day it is.

I go out on deck in time to help Del tie up the dinghy.
He has arrived from the breakwater with a fat string of

fish — five calico bass, four rock bass, two sculpins, and a fish that looks a little like a croaker but is not. All of them weigh about a pound and a half apiece. Besides the fish he has brought back a bucket of mussels that he has pried from the rocks.

Del is not only a fine catcher of small fish, he is also excellent at skinning and filleting. Most fishermen do not like this job, but Del does, almost as much as he likes fishing. He uses a sharp knife, a pair of gloves, and a pair of pliers, and turns out beautiful slices, thick and boneless.

The navigator is also the cook and she does well with the harvest Del has snatched from the sea. We have for supper a heaping platter of bass dusted with dry mustard (mustard is the secret) and fried quickly in deep fat. The mussels are steamed and set down in a ring of fluffed rice and covered with a thick sauce made of tomatoes and sweet pimentos. French bread, buttered, wrapped in foil and steamed, completes the meal, except for scoops of pineapple sherbet. We make up for a breakfast of orange juice and doughnuts, a lunch of jelly and peanut butter sandwiches.

Rod eats heartily but fast and before the rest of us are finished asks to be excused. He is dressed in his sharpest seagoing outfit. As he goes past me on his way out, he pauses to ask for an advance on his wages.

"I gave you money yesterday," I remind him.

"I need more. We are going up to Laguna Beach."

"We," I assume, is the girl in the boat next door. I don't want to give him too much money in advance for fear that he will jump ship. I would like to keep him until we reach San Francisco, where it will be easier to find someone to take his place. But under the glow of his melting blue eyes and white-tooth smile I soften and hand over twenty dollars.

"If it's clear in the morning, we'll varnish," I tell him. "Aye, aye, Captain," he replies, giving me a smart salute as he disappears.

Captain Thompson

4

There is a light fog in the morning, which quickly burns off, but the wood that Rod has sanded is damp. We decide to layover for another day and varnish in the afternoon. The varnish will be dry by nightfall and we could leave then for San Pedro, our next port, but I don't like to travel along the coast at night in heavy traffic.

The decision works out well. Del goes to fish off the breakwater, while I read; Elizabeth has a chance to do some swimming in water that is warmer than the open sea; and Rod invites his new girl aboard, the two of them taking over the flydeck.

The girl's name is Diane. She is long-legged like her namesake and has long blond hair that the sun has faded out to the color of taffy. She plays a guitar and moans sad songs. Rod looks handsome in peppermint-striped swim trunks and he dives well, doing good half gainers off the flydeck from time to time.

"You must have won some medals for your diving," I

say when he climbs out of the water and passes me as I sit in the stern with Dana's book in my hand.

"Not so much for diving as swimming," Rod says.

"Sprints or distance?" I ask, sorry now that I have said anything.

"Both," he says, "but mostly distance."

After his next dive from the flydeck, he launches off on a sweep of the harbor, swimming a powerful stroke. He returns a little out of breath but looking like a Greek god who has just swum the Hellespont.

I thumb through Dana's book and find the place where he tells about a Kanaka, a Hawaiian swimmer he once knew, who went after a ship as it left the harbor and swam so fast that he caught it.

The next time Rod dives and climbs back on board I give him the book and point out this story about the Kanaka. He reads it quickly, riffles through the book, then hands it back, pointing out a piece he wants me to read — to my astonishment! He dives again and while he is gone I look at the passage, though I have read it many times before.

"For several days," writes Dana, "the captain seemed very very much out of humor. Nothing went right, or fast enough for him . . . But his displeasure was chiefly turned against a large, heavy-moulded fellow from the Middle states, who was called Sam. This man hesitated in his speech, and was rather slow in his motions . . . The captain found fault with everything this man did . . .

"We worked late Friday night and were turned to,

early Saturday morning. About ten o'clock the captain ordered our new officer, Russell, who by this time had become thoroughly disliked by all the crew, to get the gig ready to take him ashore. John, the Swede, who was the best sailor on board, was sitting in the boat alongside, and Russell and myself were standing by the main hatchway, waiting for the captain who was down in the hold, where the crew were at work, when we heard his voice raised in violent dispute . . .

" 'You see your condition. You see your condition. Will you ever give me any more of your jaw?' . . .

" 'I never give you any, sir,' said Sam; for it was his voice that we heard, though low and half-choked.

" 'That's not what I ask you. Will you ever be impudent to me again?'

" 'I never have been, sir,' said Sam.

" 'Answer my question, or I'll make a spread eagle of you!'

" 'I'm no Negro slave,' said Sam.

" 'Then I'll make you one,' said the captain, and he came to the hatchway, and sprang on deck, threw off his coat, and rolling up his sleeves, called out to the mate — 'Seize that man up, Mr. Amerzene! Seize him up! Make a spread eagle of him! . . . '

"The crew and officers followed the captain up the hatchway, and after repeated orders the mate laid hold of Sam, who made no resistance, and carried him to the gangway.

" 'What are you going to flog the man for, sir?' said John, the Swede, to the captain.

"Upon hearing this, the captain turned upon him, but

knowing him to be quick and resolute, he ordered the steward to bring the irons, and calling upon Russell to help him, went up to John.

"'Let me alone,' said John. 'I'm willing to be put in irons. You need not use any force'; and putting out his hands, the captain slipped the irons on, and sent him aft to the quarter-deck.

"Sam by this time was seized up, as it is called, that is, placed against the shrouds, with his arms spread out and his wrists made fast to the shrouds, his jacket off, and his back exposed. The captain stood on the break of the deck, a few feet from him, and a little raised, so as to have a good swing at him, and held in his hand the bight of a thick, strong rope. The officers stood around, and the crew grouped together in the waist . . .

"Swinging the rope over his head, and bending his body so as to give it full force, the captain brought it down upon the poor fellow's back. Once, twice, — six times.

" 'Will you ever give me any more of your jaw?'

"The man writhed with pain, but said not a word. Three times more. This was too much, and he muttered something which I could not hear; this brought as many more as the man could stand; when the captain ordered him to be cut down . . .

" 'Now for you,' said the captain, making up to John and taking his irons off. As soon as he was loose, he ran forward onto the forecastle. 'Bring that man aft,' shouted the captain.

"The captain stood on the quarter-deck, bareheaded, his eyes flashing with rage, and his face as red as blood, swinging the rope and calling out to his officers, 'Drag him aft! Lay hold of him! I'll sweeten him.'

"The mate now went forward and told John quietly to go aft . . .

"When he was made fast, he turned to the captain, who stood turning up his sleeves and getting ready for the blow, and asked him what he was to be flogged for.

" 'Have I ever refused my duty, sir? Have you ever known me to hang back, or to be insolent, or not to know my work?'

" 'No,' said the captain, 'it is not that that I flog you for; I flog you for your interference — for asking questions.'

"'Can't a man ask questions here without being flogged?'

"'No,' shouted the captain; 'nobody shall open his mouth aboard this vessel, but myself'; and began laying the blows upon his back, swinging half around between each blow, to give it full effect . . .

"The man writhed under the pain, until he could endure it no longer, when he called out — 'Oh, Jesus Christ! Oh, Jesus Christ!'

" 'Don't call on Jesus Christ,' shouted the captain, 'he can't help you. Call on Frank Thompson! He's the man! He can help you! Jesus Christ can't help you now!'

"At these words, which I shall never forget, my blood ran cold . . .

" 'You see your condition! You see where I've got you all, and you know what to expect! You've been mistaken in me — you didn't know what I was! Now you know what I am! I'll make you toe the mark, every soul of you, or I'll flog you all, fore and aft, from the boy, up! . . .'

"Soon after, John came aft, with his bare back covered with stripes and wales in every direction, and dreadfully swollen, and asked the steward to ask the captain to let him have some salve, or balsam, to put upon it.

" 'No,' said the captain, who heard him from below, 'tell him to put his shirt on; that's the best thing for him; and pull me ashore in the boat. Nobody is going to lay-up on board this vessel."

I finish reading as Rod climbs on deck and stands over me in his peppermint-colored trunks, dripping water. He wants to know what I think of the passage.

"The part that gets me," I say, "is right at the last when Captain Thompson has stripped the flesh from John's back and then has John row him ashore."

"What gets me," Rod says, "is that neither John nor Sam did anything about the floggings. They rowed Thompson ashore and then went off and sat on a rock."

"What could they do?" I ask. "If they had fought Thompson, it would be mutiny. And if they got help from the crew and seized the ship, they'd be strung up for pirates."

"Well, there have been mutineers and pirates all through history. And, man, many of them have been very successful," Rod says with a smile.

I am more puzzled about him than I was before. I am surprised that he has read a book, a good one besides, and I wonder why, with all the passages he could have chosen for me to read, he chose the one about Captain Thompson. Does he think that I am a slave driver? Do I remind him in some way of Captain Thompson?

I suddenly recall that some of the topside has not been varnished and I gently remind him of the fact.

"It's getting pretty late in the day for varnish," he replies. "It won't dry before night, man."

"Let's take a chance," I say, determined to get the job done, even though I may sound like Captain Thompson.

"What about Del?" he asks. "Why can't he do a little sanding, too?"

"Del is not getting paid," I answer. "He's a guest."

"Nothing wrong with a guest doing a little work, is there?"

"It's up to Del, what he wants to do."

Rod abandons the argument. He straightens up and gives me a smart salute. "Aye, aye," he says, speaking in the sonorous tones of Charles Laughton and with a thick British accent. "I'll have a go at it. But don't blame me if the varnish flakes off in a couple of days."

"I won't blame you," I say. "If it flakes off, then you can varnish it again."

"Aye, aye, Sir."

Sir?

FIVE

The Navigator

1

MORNING DAWNS WINDLESS and clear and you can see the crests of blue gray islands off to the southwest. We bring in the anchor and move out into mid-channel, headed for San Pedro.

"What's our reading?" I ask my wife, the navigator. She has a chart spread out on the dining table and is working with dividers and a parallel ruler.

"Two hundred and eighty," she says.

When I reach the end of the breakwater, I turn the wheel until the compass reads two hundred and eighty degrees.

"What's our Estimated Time of Arrival?"

"At what speed?"

"Ten knots," I say and rev up the engine to 1600 RPMs.

The navigator figures on a pad, checks her figures and

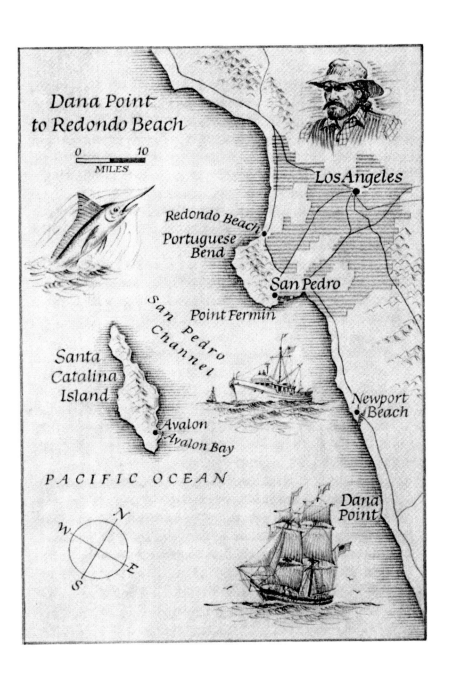

Dana Point
to Redondo Beach

0   10
MILES

Redondo Beach
Portuguese
Bend

Los Angeles

San Pedro

Point Fermin

San Pedro Channel

Santa
Catalina
Island

Avalon
Avalon Bay

Newport
Beach

PACIFIC OCEAN

N
W   E
S

Dana
Point

says, "The E.T.A. is twenty minutes after one, to the breakwater light."

When we first got the boat, I did all the navigating, since I had had prior experience on the sea and had even served a hitch in the Coast Guard Auxiliary. To improve my skills, since it is one thing to work with a crew and something else to handle a seagoing boat practically alone, I enrolled for a Coast Guard course in seamanship, taught at the Coast Guard station in San Diego. I went two evenings a week, and my wife went along, dutifully, thinking she might pick up some information that would help me handle the boat.

We went to every class and at the end of three months we took the two-hour test for the Coast Guard Auxiliary's Certificate of Merit. My wife felt shaky about what she had learned and did not want to take the test.

"I'm sure I'll fail."

"You'll do better than you think," I comforted her.

And she did, though it turned out to be a very difficult test. There were fifty questions about who has the right of way and how to tie a bowline and what a black nun marker means, and they counted for fifty points. But another fifty points were given for the right answer to one very complicated question in navigation.

The question went something like this: You leave San Diego harbor at seven in the morning. You travel due west for an hour and ten minutes at eight knots. At this time you take your bearings, using two landmarks on the coast. With this bearing you plot a course for Avalon Bay at Santa Catalina and give your E.T.A. After two hours and twenty minutes on this course, you plot a new course for Newport Harbor, and now travel at seven knots. Give your heading and E.T.A. for Newport Harbor.

The examination lasted two hours. Elizabeth finished her paper in less than an hour and looked discouraged as she handed it in. I begged her to relax and take more time and go over the paper again, but she refused.

Thirty-two of us took the test. Of the thirty-two, twenty failed and I was one of the twenty. Elizabeth answered all the questions correctly, got one hundred percent, the only perfect score in the class.

That is why she is now the navigator, and when she says that we will arrive off the San Pedro light at 1:20, I believe her.

Brown Pelican

2

The weather report has promised us light swells of two feet at intervals of twelve seconds, but the sea is flat. We pass a flock of gulls floating on the water, as still as if they were perched on a rock. There are no boats in sight and I can see clearly for twenty miles or more. I could see even farther, to the hills beyond San Pedro, if it weren't for a streamer of sulfurous brown smog that trails out from Los Angeles and curls back over the sea.

Stone cliffs rise to starboard and lazy waves are breaking against them. Flocks of small gray and white birds skitter over the kelp beds, but I miss the pelicans.

Two years ago when you sailed along this part of the coast early in the morning, you would always find them skimming the sea, ten or twelve birds in a flight. They flew without moving their wings, in a long glide and one after the other, along the line of the surf where the waves were just beginning to crest, so close to the water that they were at times covered with spray, touching the water now and again with the tips of their wings, so close that you marveled when they did not crash. It seemed that they were not searching for food, nor were they on their way anywhere. It was a flight of pure joy.

Once I held one of these birds while a broken wing was being placed in a splint. She filled my arms, not counting the long bill that was snapping open and shut in my face with a sound like the clashing of bamboo swords, yet she was as light as a feather pillow. Sitting on a pier or afloat, brown pelicans look clownish, but as they glide over the water these great-winged birds are beautiful. It disturbs me that we are killing them off with our deadly insecticides, which saturate the sea and make their eggs so fragile that they will not hatch.

The automatic pilot has been warming up for five minutes, which is a good thing. Holding the wheel until I get the correct bearing on the compass, keeping it there until I am sure that the boat will hold this position of two hundred eighty degrees, allowing for the slight back and forth movement of the wheel, I pull out the knob that turns the boat over to the judgment and care of the automatic pilot. No helmsman can steer better than this small but complicated device, except in a storm. It is affectionately known to sailors as Iron Mike.

Steering is fun. It is not like steering a car. With your hands on the helm you become a part of the sea — the wind and waves and the currents. The feel of the sea comes to you through the heavy bronze rudder and the steel cables that fasten it to the wheel. But it comes, too, in a more subtle way. With the lightest touch if the day is calm, with a bang if the day is stormy. There is ever-changing life in the sea and a boat gathers it in and gives it over to the helmsman.

It is also fun just to sit and think, while Iron Mike does the work.

Mountain Man

3

When I think of Jedediah Smith, the greatest of the mountain men, I never think of him sailing north from San Diego in an attempt to escape from the Mexican governor of California, who was very anxious to throw him in jail. A more interesting story is how he got to California in the first place.

Jed, the first white man to cross the continent from the Missouri River to California, was born of adventurous stock. His great-great-great grandfather was an Indian fighter and was killed by the Indians. An uncle went to sea on a sailing brig and never returned. His grandfather was famous because he alone in all of history — though quite by accident — went over Niagara Falls with no protection of any kind and lived to tell the tale.

In the spring of 1822, Jed arrived in St. Louis by keel-boat. He was twenty-three and had come from Ohio, stirred to his boots by a book he had read called the *Journals of Lewis and Clark.* In a few weeks he had signed on with fur trader General Ashley and was on his way to the west.

Jed had given away his homespun Ohio clothes and now wore woolen leggings and the buckskin shirt of the hunter. His long hair fell to his shoulders, his face was clean-shaven. In a plunder bag he carried the Bible he read every night and his writing materials. The writing materials were important because he planned to keep a careful record of all that he did and saw, so when he came back he could sit down and make an atlas of the Shining Mountains and the wondrous country that lay beyond, a map for everyone to marvel at.

But first off, he was going to make money for his mother and father and all the children — there were four-teen of them including himself — and then maybe if the Indians didn't lift his scalp, he would have a house some-day as big as the house General Ashley lived in.

The White Grizzly

4

Jed followed Ashley's brigade into the Rocky Moun-tains. He worked out of the fort at Yellowstone, made winter camp in the Musselshell. He built bullboats out of stretched hides on sapling frames that looked like upside-down umbrellas, gathered beaver pelts and sold them at the spring rendezvous. After this meeting of traders and trappers, he traveled wide, writing down in his journal what he saw.

He learned that some Indians shot white men on sight, and that others could be friendly one minute and treacherous the next. He knew what it was to be frozen and to go without water for days. He knew where the beaver were. He fought the Blackfeet and saw his friends fall around him in a battle with the Arikara. He became a seasoned mountain man and the leader of a small brigade. Ashley called him Captain Smith.

The brigade was traveling west from Fort Kiowa one morning in fine weather, moving along as usual in single file, in a creek bottom covered with brush. Usually the horses would sense danger before the men did, be it Indians or a rattlesnake.

"Grizzly!" shouted Tom Fitzpatrick. "Grizzly bear!"

At his shout a full-grown grizzly burst forth from the brush. He was big and mean-looking and white and he came charging toward the center of the moving brigade. The horses reacted first by galloping out of his path.

Grizzly bears will move away from danger as a rule. But if they are cornered or think that they are cornered, or if they are simply out of sorts, they will stand and fight. If they are angry they will not only stand but they will also chase anything that lives on earth. This grizzly was angry.

Jed was riding up front at the head of the line, looking over the country that lay ahead, when Fitzpatrick's shout reached his ears. Jed was no more afraid of a grizzly than any other mountain man, but that fear was considerable. In fact, of all the dangers that lurked on the frontier, even the danger of Indians, grizzly bears were feared the most.

Jed spurred his horse up a short rise, hoping to get an idea of what was happening behind him, where the bear was, and what he was doing. At that moment, as he rode into the open, the grizzly rushed out upon him.

There are no small bears; the smallest are twice as big as a man. The grizzly can weigh half a ton and when he rears on his hind legs he can stand twice as tall as a tall man. For his weight, he is agile and swift.

The grizzly made one leap, and for a second of time Jed and the beast were face to face. Before Jed could move, before he could reach for the rifle that was in a holster under his leg or for the pistol tucked in his belt, the grizzly's mouth gaped open and snapped shut on his head. It stayed shut for a moment, then for some reason opened, and Jed fell to the ground, blinded by blood and his own scalp that had been torn apart.

Stunned, he lay sprawled on the ground. Again the bear leaped upon him, striking this time for his stomach. Its fangs held fast on his middle, but by chance had struck his bullet pouch and butcher knife and did not sink in.

Jed's comrades had come up meanwhile and were circling about him, their rifles primed and ready. But the grizzly, its great mouth still clamped shut, was holding Jed in such a way that no one could shoot without fear of killing him.

In desperation Black Harris finally moved closer, got an angle from which he thought he might be able to shoot, took careful aim, and pulled the trigger. Struck in a vital spot, the grizzly reared back, clawed the air, and fell dead.

Clyman and Black Harris stared down in horror at their comrade. They had never seen a man so badly mauled, even by Indians. They looked at each other.

Jim Clyman knelt beside Jed and put a hand on his arm. "What will we do, Cap'n?" he said.

What is there to do? Black Harris thought, still staring down at the mangled face of his friend.

Jed opened his eyes and looked up. "Get me some water," he whispered.

Two of the men started off for a stream they had passed some time before.

Jed spoke again. "Jim, get your needle and thread and sew my wounds up," he said.

Wondering how he ever could close Jed's gaping flesh, Clyman ran for his saddlebag and fished out thread and needle.

They turned Jed over on his back and washed away the blood on his face. They cut his long hair and washed it. As Jim Clyman knelt and held the threaded needle, his hand began to shake. It shook until he saw that Jed was lying quiet and without fear, waiting for him to begin.

Jim Clyman was not a doctor but he managed to lay the edges of the ragged flesh one against the other and slowly, taking his time, forced the needle through and brought the edges together. He did this again and again, one wound after another, until every wound had been sewed up. Except for an ear that dangled from a single shred of flesh.

Clyman shook his head. "Cap'n, I can't do nothing for yore ear. "

Jed did not move. He wanted his ear. "Put it together somehow," he said. "Do the best you can, Jim."

Jim Clyman gritted his teeth and went at the job again, arranging the shreds and fastening them together so that they looked something like an ear. He spread buffalo tallow over all the wounds and bandaged them with pads of muslin and buffalo wool.

Jed sat up then and took a drink of water and started to get on his feet.

"We'll carry you," Black Harris said.

"I can ride, if it isn't far," Jed answered.

They brought up his horse, helped him into the saddle, and led him back to the stream, where they put up their tent and laid Jed in it. No one thought he would live out the day. They stood around and waited, saying little to each other.

Jed lived through that day and night, through the second day and the second night. He asked for food and grew stronger. At the end of a week, climbing into the saddle, he led his brigade of mountain men slowly into the west.

Ambush on the Mojave

5

Captain Jed Smith had long thought of traveling into California. Little was known about this country which belonged to the Mexicans, to the Spaniards before them. But he was certain that there would be fine trapping in the Mexican streams, many wondrous things to be seen, to tell about, and to put down in his journal.

In August of 1826, with seventeen men, he left Great Salt Lake and struck out for California.

Jed was now twenty-seven years old and he had been on the frontier for more than four years. In that short time he had worked his way up from a meat hunter and clerk to the captain of a brigade. Confident of his powers, he then had bought out his employers and become the commander of three hundred mountain men.

Jed looked much the same as when he had started out from St. Louis, except for his face that the bear had scarred. He still wore his long hair tied in a bandana knotted at the back, fringed buckskin from shoulder to knee, and red woolen hose (buckskin leggings shrank when wet and caused their owner severe pain). In his plunder bag he still carried his Bible and his journal. The only thing he had added to it was the paw of the white grizzly that had come near to killing him.

The brigade of eighteen men and fifty horses and mules, each man riding and leading one or more animals, crossed the Colorado River and the Mojave Desert. In the last week of November, having been on the trail for three months, the ragged and half-starved brigade climbed to the summit of Cajon Pass and looked down upon a sweeping valley lush with grass from early rains, where thousands of cattle grazed. The Pacific Ocean lay to the west.

Jed received a friendly welcome from the fathers at

Mission San Gabriel. But the governor thought he looked and acted like a spy and ordered him out of the country. (This was the time when Jed sailed from San Diego to San Pedro in an effort to elude his pursuers.)

Jed liked California and he did not want to leave. He went, however, vowing that he would be back, whether the Californians liked it or not. That vow he kept.

This time he left Salt Lake with a brigade of eighteen men — mostly new recruits of French, English, Spanish, and American descent — and two Indian wives. He took about the same course as he had the year before, and without mishap arrived at the Mojave village on the Colorado River some hundred miles from the southern boundary of California.

Jed found the Mojaves shy at first, but he coaxed them with gifts and they became as friendly as they had been the last time he had visited the village. If anything they seemed friendlier, laughing and joking while they bartered beaver pelts and dried pumpkin for beads.

The Mojaves helped the brigade to move its supplies across the river, using rafts woven of reeds. On a sandbar that jutted out from the west bank Jed stacked the goods as the rafts brought them in. At the same time the horse guards were swimming the stock across.

The guards had just ridden out of the river and were talking to Jed when two hundred and more Mojaves burst out of a willow thicket. Armed with arrows, spears, and clubs, their faces painted with red and white slashes, they fell screaming upon the brigade.

The battle was brief. Within moments more than half of the mountain men were cut down and lay dead or dying on the sandbar, in the river, on the far bank. One by one, without exception, they then were scalped and mutilated, and the horses and booty and the two Indian wives were borne away.

By some miracle of chance, Jed and eight of his men survived the ambush and rallied on the sandbar. Jed knew that they had no chance against such an overwhelming foe, but he would not give up. He would not let them stand and wait to be killed in cold blood.

Weighing the circumstances, he talked his men into scattering their belongings on the sandbar, which they did.
"The Indians will fight over them," he said, "and while they're fighting we'll have a chance to make a run for it. If there's anything you want or think you can use, take it now."

There were five rifles left and some knives and these the men took. Jed hoisted a sack of dried beef to his shoulder and they all set off, running at a trot through the hot sand. They had not gone a mile when Jed heard yells from nearby and saw that the Indians were gathering for another attack.

"Run for the river," he shouted, and pointed to a grove of cottonwoods growing on the bank. "Run for your lives."

They fled back to the river. Here with the wide Colorado behind them they would have a better chance of defending themselves.

In the midst of the thicket of young cottonwoods the brigade cut a small place where they could stand and put up a crude breastwork of trees in front of it, facing the enemy. They had five rifles but only a small amount of powder and shot, so Jed had the men bind their butcher knives to the ends of cottonwood boles, making lances like those the Californians used.

"Don't fire more than three rifles at once," Jed told them. "Don't fire unless you are sure you will hit your mark."

Behind the flimsy barricade of cottonwoods, Jed watched the Mojaves mount their attack. In a wide crescent, screaming taunts as they dodged from cover to cover, they drew closer, taking their time as if they enjoyed toying with their prey.

Jed was aware that he held one advantage over the Indians. The Mojave's chief weapon was the bow and arrow, and though they had seen the American rifle, they did not understand that it could kill at a distance. In truth, they held it in contempt.

He waited patiently, cautioning his men to hold their fire, watching the painted warriors draw closer. He waited until three of the Indians drew bold enough to jump out in the open, brandishing their bows. The distance was long, but Jed told his best two marksmen to take careful aim and to fire, told a third marksman to be ready.

The amazement of the Mojaves was great when two of the cavorting Indians lurched and lay still. Their amazement was greater yet when the third Indian slumped in the sand. Everywhere there was quiet. Then came a wail of fright and frustration, and hundreds of warriors scurried away out of range and out of view.

Jed waited. He was still uncertain whether or not the

Mojaves would rally their warriors and return to the fight. He waited in the cottonwood thicket until night fell and then led his brigade on a fast march toward the west.

Days later, half-alive, the brigade went through Cajon Pass and down the western slope. Within two years Jed had made his second trip into California. Ratelle and Robiseau lay behind him on the Colorado, also Gobel, Ortega, Cunningham, Pale, Polita, Deramme, and Campbell. These of his men were dead, but a path had been plainly marked for other men to see.

SIX

Sink or Swim

1

POINT FERMIN LIGHT is flashing as we drop the anchor. We are five hours behind the E.T.A., but it is not the fault of our navigator. Toward noon we slowed down to let Del troll again for swordfish. He had no luck, but as long as he has a pole in his hand he is happy.

The hills above the harbor are strung with lights that wind around in an ascending ring, upward and upward. They look like a giant Christmas tree and the reflections shine on the water and across our deck. The breakwater protects us from the wind, so we have supper on the flydeck, using the small hibachi to broil hamburgers, heat up a pot of frijoles with red chilies, and toast tortillas.

I have not seen San Pedro for a long time, not since I was a boy. My family moved to the town when I was eight years old, and the day we came I went down to the harbor with the boys on my street. We went to the wharf on the north side of the channel, where the water was deep enough to dive without hitting your head on a rock. In fact, the water was twenty feet deep at low tide. It was the deepest water I had ever seen.

The other boys skinned out of their clothes and stood around naked waiting for me to skin out of mine. I took my time at this, for underneath my clothes I had on a swimming suit, which my mother had made me wear. It was called a swimming suit because that was really what it looked like — a top with short sleeves and a bottom with legs that reached almost to my knees.

I must have looked pretty funny standing there on the wharf in my red swimming suit, with my skinny arms and legs sticking out, but no one laughed. All they did was stare, which was understandable, since they had never seen a swimming suit before, nor — being the husky, dark-skinned sons of Italian and Portuguese fishermen — a skinny Anglo-Saxon with white skin. They all stared and then after a while looked away.

Then one of them gave me an up and down glance and said, "Can you swim?" Considering the way I looked, this was not a foolish question. The boy who asked the question was named Jack Iman. He was my age and height but he was twice my size, a small Hercules, with a bang of black hair hanging on his forehead and a splattering of black freckles.

I had never been in water more than waist-deep before and I had never swum, unless flailing your arms while crouching with one foot firmly on the bottom can be called swimming. But how could I confess this to the boys who lived on Elm Street, the street I had just moved into, who I hoped would be my friends someday? They had invited me to go swimming and I had come down to the wharf with them and here I was in my red swimming suit.

I was standing on a plank that ran along the edge of the wharf. The water was very clear and I could see smelt darting about and far down in the depths, at least twenty feet down, some sort of a small shark moving along the sandy bottom.

Two of the boys dove off the wharf. Two more followed and I heard them hit the water.

Jack Iman stepped up beside me on the plank. "How's it?" he called down to the boys who were now treading water.

I did not hear what they said. I was hoping that Jack Iman had forgotten about me, that he might jump in the water and I might quietly disappear. When I met him again I could say that I had been seized by a stomachache and had to go home. I might even tell the truth and say that I could not swim.

Jack Iman looked at me again. Two more of the boys jumped off the wharf. Jack looked at me for a long time. Then he turned his back, leaned over the edge of the wharf, and dove. I saw him strike the water and slant downward in a trail of bubbles.

In the few seconds before he rose to the surface I made up my mind. It came to me in a flash. I was not going to run back home with an imaginary ache in my stomach, nor was I going to say that I could not swim. I would rather drown in twenty feet of water than do either.

I jumped and fell through the air holding my breath,

my eyes closed, too scared to pray. It was not a dive of any sort, nor was it graceful. It was more as if someone had given me a push. I fell and fell but I reached the water, nevertheless, belly first and gasping, righted myself, and from pure instinct, like a dog, I made for a piling where I clung until I got my breath and could climb back on the wharf up the crude ladder the boys had built.

No one applauded my performance, as I remember the scene now, nor did anyone laugh. I guess everyone was just happy that the new boy on Elm Street had not drowned.

Gila Monster

2

I know that San Pedro has changed since then. I have read about the harbor and seen pictures of it, but it remains to me what it is in memory — a few narrow streets crowding the waterfront, with saloons on every corner and in the middle of every block. Sailing ships anchored close in, and above the town were hills that we called Palos Verdes, which were really only one hill with a rounded top.

But it was a big hill and from the top you could look down the coast and see the mountains of Mexico. You could see the ocean as it swung around Point Fermin and past the breakwater and into the channel between Dead Man's Island and San Pedro, making a harbor that was small yet deep enough for sailing ships.

We climbed the hill that I cannot see now — only the tiers of lights climbing out of the dark water to the darker sky. We went up the hill on Saturday mornings, unless it rained, twelve of us in a gang, about half girls and half boys.

The girls gathered wildflowers if there were any in bloom, but usually they gathered bunches of ferns in a small canyon where people went to dig gravel. There were always ferns of some kind, the lacy maidenhair and the coffee fern and the one that looked like a spear and was called a sword fern.

Sometimes there were cactus apples for the girls to gather. They were best to eat when they had turned a deep red, almost purple, but you could eat them any time, even when they were half-green, and this we did if we had to.

The girls not only gathered cactus apples but they also got them ready to eat. This took patience and skill and good luck. First the boys built a fire, then the girls speared the apples with a sharp stick and held them against the flames until all the spines were burned off. The spines on a cactus apple are more numerous than those on a porcupine. They are smaller, of course, and as fine as a baby's hair, but they are stiff and sharp and arranged in little tufts over the whole surface. Animals cannot eat cactus apples, and wise people do not unless this spiny armor has been removed.

The flesh of the cactus apple is yellow or pink or red, depending upon how ripe it is, sprinkled with small seeds, and has a flavor of its own.

With the cactus apples we ate squirrel roasted over the

fire. This was the variety that lives in a burrow, has a long, seedy tail, a thin body, and a lot of bones. I was the only member of our gang who did not like this combination. Three days following my first meal on cactus apples and roasted ground squirrel I came down with a head-to-foot case of hives. After that I always took a sandwich along on these Saturday picnics and secretly ate it while pretending to like what the others ate.

The boys did a lot of searching. We turned over every likely rock, looking for small monsters. We thrust our hands down every squirrel and coyote hole in our path, always on the lookout for rattlesnakes. There were some on Dead Man's Island and a lot on Rattlesnake Island, but very few on the way to the gravel pit. Indeed, we killed only one rattler in all the time we went on these picnics, and that was by chance.

This event took place shortly after a medicine man came to town and put up his stand on Main Street. He had a catchy spiel but the great attraction was a gila monster which he kept in a glass cage. It looked scaly, though it did not have scales. It was squat and fat and barred with yellow and black and looked like an overgrown lizard. It had a black tongue, not a thin one like a lizard's, but a thick tongue that seemed to take up all the room in its mouth.

The medicine man cautioned us not to get too close to the cage. The gila monster, he said, had a deadly bite. Once it had its fangs into you it would never let go. To pry it loose from your flesh, it was necessary to cut its head off. The gila monster fascinated me (as a matter of fact, it still does) and during the week it was in our town I went to see it every day after school.

It seems logical therefore that when the gang went off on the next Saturday morning to pick ferns and search coyote holes, I had the monstrous lizard on my mind. And logical that when I saw a movement in the grass beside the trail and a flash of yellow and brown, I thought at once that by some miracle I had stumbled upon a gila monster.

But what happened next was not logical. I should have jumped. I should have run. Considering the gila monster's deadly bite, the fact that it never released its victim until its head had been cut off I should have done both — jumped and run at the same time.

What I did was not meant to show off in front of the girls, of which I was capable. It was not meant in a spirit of adventure, nor from bravery. I did it because what brains I possessed were suddenly addled by the thought of killing a gila monster.

I was the only one who had seen the flash of brown and yellow. Stealthily I crept forward through the knee-high grass, put my foot on the monster's back, afraid that it would run away, and called for a rock.

By the time the rock arrived, the monster had wiggled from under my foot, though I pressed down hard (I forgot to say that my shoes were at home), hard upon its back with my bare foot.

"There it is," Tom Burton shouted, handing me a rock and pointing to a place ten feet away. "It's a snake."

And so it was, a three-foot rattler with five buttons.

Any other time a rattlesnake would have been a prize. But not on this morning, with dreams of a gila monster floating around in my empty head.

I killed the rattler, skinned it on a log, and divided the skin even Stephen with Tom because he had brought the rock. When I got home I salted the skin and tacked it to the barn door. When the skin was properly cured, I planned to make a hatband of it. But sometime that night the family cat got up and dragged the skin away.

Dead Man's Island

3

I am up early the next morning and climb to the fly-deck, anxious to learn if all the places I remember have gone. I know from the newspapers that Dead Man's Island was blown up years ago, dredged out and carted away to make room for something.

It is gone all right, just as the newspapers said. I try to locate where it was by looking around for the yellow cliffs I remember. If I can find the cliffs then I can make a sighting and come close to telling where the island stood. But the yellow cliffs also are gone, leveled off and covered up by roads and warehouses.

Dead Man's Island was not a large island. You could walk around it in twenty minutes. It had no springs or palm trees, nor, as a matter of truth, trees of any kind. Ice plant and a few hardy shrubs grew there, close to the earth as if to hide as best they could from the salt winds that swept in from the Pacific. But the island fascinated me.

It fascinated Richard Henry Dana, too. His ship anchored in San Pedro harbor frequently and its longboat passed the island many times while taking on hides.

"The only thing that broke the surface of the great bay," Dana wrote in *Two Years before the Mast*, "was a small, desolate-looking island, steep and conical, of a clayey soil, and without the sign of vegetable life upon it; yet which had a peculiar and melancholy interest to me, for on top of it were buried the remains of an Englishman, the commander of a small merchant brig, who died while lying in this port.

"It was always a solemn and interesting spot to me. There it stood, desolate, and in the midst of desolation; and there were the remains of one who died and was buried alone and friendless . . . Then, too, the man died far from home . . . by poison, it was suspected."

I had not read Dana's book when I was a boy in San Pedro, but this description of how the island got its name was not exactly the one my companions and I were familiar with. If there were poison connected with the captain's death, it was not given to him by the ship's mate, as Dana suggests, but by the crew, who were bent upon finding a chest of Spanish gold that had come into the captain's possession. Where it came from no one seemed to know, but that it was filled with gold in the form of doubloons was certain.

Sometime during the first night *Betsy Anne* was anchored in the harbor (as we heard the story from Sam Walker, an English sailor) a longboat drew abreast, manned by four Spanish soldiers. They hailed the captain and carried the leather chest, which was so heavy that it required the strength of all four men, up the ladder and into his cabin.

During the next day there was much conjecture among the members of the crew about it. Nothing, some said, could be put into a chest that took four men to lift, except gold. One of the crew said that he had heard the ringing sound of gold coins striking together as the chest was placed down in the captain's quarters.

There were questions, too, about where the gold had come from and into whose pocket it would go. The fact that soldiers in the uniform of Spain had brought it to the ship indicated that the treasure belonged to the king of Spain. It could belong to the Spanish viceroy in Mexico, since the ship planned to stop in Acapulco, which was the port of Mexico City. No one thought that the doubloons belonged to the captain. And there was not a sailor on the *Betsy Anne* who did not scheme to get his hands on them.

Captain Mulvaney must have been aware of the talk and the scheming that went on during the day. He must have realized then that it would be folly for him to try to sail out of the harbor without an armed guard to protect the chest.

Sometime toward midnight and again near dawn the captain rowed away from the ship in one of the longboats. The man on watch saw him leave both times and thought that he had gone ashore; at least he had headed in that direction. The captain made two more trips away from the ship on the following night, again toward shore.

While he was gone on the last trip, three of the crew went to Captain Mulvaney's cabin, but found the door locked. The ship's carpenter, who was good at picking locks, was summoned. The carpenter managed the job, and the four men entered the cabin just as the longboat bearing the captain approached.

After a hasty search they located the leather chest and flung back the lid, only to find that the chest was empty. The captain's heels sounded on the deck and the men were quickly turning away when one of them saw, deep in a recess of the chest, the gleam of a gold coin. He stopped, dug the coin out, and the four men fled, in their hurry leaving the chest open.

The coin, they learned when they reached the forecastle and examined it under lantern light, was a gold doubloon minted in the city of Lima, Peru, in the year 1691, bearing a design of two towers and a dove flying.

The coin proved what most of the men were sure of already. But where were the rest of the doubloons? Where had the captain hidden them? He had left the ship four times, each time apparently burdened down with all the coins he could carry. Had he hidden the treasure in the sand? Had he turned it over to someone, an accomplice who was waiting for him on the shore? The ship seethed with questions.

Next morning, aware that some of the crew had entered his cabin and fearing mutiny if he stayed in the harbor, the captain gave orders to ready the ship for sailing. The crew obeyed, but went about their duties in a bad spirit, angry that now they would not have a chance to get their hands on the gold doubloons.

At this point Sam Walker, the old Englishman who told us how the island got its name, would pause. Sam told us the story many times, whenever we found him on the wharf and in a happy mood, and he always paused when he came to the place where the captain ordered the crew to make the ship ready to sail.

Sam had a bad eye and a limp and one arm was cut off at the wrist and had an iron hook attached to it. He looked exactly like Long John Silver, except for the patch. I was reading *Treasure Island* at the time — I was always reading *Treasure Island* — and every time that Sam Walker would tell stories, I would feel that I was listening to Long John Silver.

"My grandfather, Mark Walker, was a member of that mutinous crew," Sam would continue. "You will recall that he was a man with a remarkable memory — he could recite half the Bible by heart — yet he could never remember exactly what happened next. Whether the anchor was being hauled in, or whether it was already hauled and the ship was moving away on the tide."

"Anyway, it happened," Jack Iman would say, or something like it, impatient for the old man to get on with the story. "What's the diff?"

"Yes, moving or not, what's the diff?" Sam agreed.

"It would make a big difference," I said, speaking more to Jack Iman than to the Englishman, "if the ship was moving and ran on the rocks while the crew was busy fighting the captain."

"Well, it didn't run on the rocks," Jack Iman said, and that would end that and we would be quiet and wait for the old man to go on.

It appears — what he told us each time was always the same — that while the ship was still anchored or under way, whichever, the crew went to the captain's quarters, first taking the precaution of tying the mate to the foremast, and knocked on the door.

Captain Mulvaney invited them in. There was room for only half the crew, and half entered the cabin and ranged themselves against the bulwarks. Their spokesman, Mark Walker, explained that they had come to ask about the gold doubloons the captain had carried away in the dark of the night, and also when their wages were to be paid.

The captain was forthright or appeared to be. He said that it was true, he had carried the treasure away.

"Where?" Mark Walker asked.

"Ashore."

"What did you do with it?"

"Left it with friends for safekeeping."

"Safekeeping? The gold was brought here only two days ago. Last night, only a day later, you and the mate take it away. What's going on, Captain Mulvaney? We have a right to know because our wages have not been paid for a month."

The captain hesitated but only a moment. "You will remember that an officer from the Spanish garrison in Los Angeles came to see me yesterday, yesterday morning."

None of the crew seemed to remember. They waited, watching the captain in silence, though they had seen the Spaniard come aboard.

"The officer brought word that the Spanish authorities

in San Diego planned to seize the gold as soon as we anchored. And we have to go to San Diego. More than thirty thousand dollars in hides, which took us four months to collect, are in the San Diego warehouse. I had no choice except to leave the gold here."

"What about our wages?" someone asked.

"You'll be paid as soon as we reach San Diego," Captain Mulvaney replied.

"Why didn't we get paid with doubloons?" Mark Walker said.

"Because the doubloons were not mine."

The crew was puzzled, puzzled about everything, angry that the prize had slipped away, angry at themselves and at the captain, at the Spaniards who ran the country. But they left and went to the forecastle, where they put their heads together to decide what to do next.

The first thing they decided was that they would not leave port until their wages were paid in full. Secondly they decided to have a talk with the mate who was still tied to the mast.

They untied him quietly and took him back to the forecastle. There, to their great surprise, when he saw that they were in a dangerous mood, that the knife at his throat might suddenly slip, the mate confessed.

"Last night," he said, "we made four trips in the longboat, Captain Mulvaney and me. You must understand, men, that I went because I was ordered. I had to. We rowed for the shore, but once out of sight of the ship we turned back and made our way to the island. A heavy wind was blowing and we couldn't land the boat, so I stayed at the oars and kept her from capsizing while the captain waded ashore with the gold. He buried it somewhere. He was gone a long time each trip we made. I think he must have climbed as far as he could go. He didn't tell me where he went. But I think he must have climbed to the very top and buried it up there."

The crew locked Captain Mulvaney in his cabin and put a guard of two men on the door. They left another guard on deck and the rest of them rowed over to the island and began a search -for the gold doubloons. They searched until dark and went back at dawn the next morning and searched all day, on the conical top of the island and along its steep sides. Finding no trace of the buried treasure, they confronted the captain while he was eating supper.

"We've been on a hunt for the gold," Mark Walker said. "We've hunted the island up and down and everywhere. Since you are the one who did the burying perhaps you can tell us where to look. It would save us a lot of time and perhaps save your neck, Captain Mulvaney, if you were just to speak up."

The captain seemed surprised. He shoved his food away and stood up. "Who told you that I buried the gold?" he demanded.

"Mr. Sparks, the mate."

"Mr. Sparks is a liar," the captain shouted. "Fetch him and I'll tell him so."

Mr. Sparks was sent for at once. As he said he would do, the captain called Sparks a liar. Whereupon Sparks called the captain a liar. The two men went at each other until the crew decided to lock them in the cabin. A guard was placed at the door and Mark Walker gave the captain and the mate instructions.

"Talk it over," he told them. "Try to make up your minds where the gold doubloons are now located and if you do, then let us know."

Captain Mulvaney and Mr. Sparks were left in the cabin and in the morning the crew split up into two parties, one searching the shore for the gold and the other continuing the search on the island. When they came back that night, unsuccessful, the cabin was quiet, but the guards who had been stationed at the door reported that the two men had been arguing most of the day, shouting at each other and knocking things about.

The crew's spokesman called through the door and asked the captain and mate if they had come to a decision. Receiving no reply, he left after telling the two men that he was in no hurry to hear from them, that they could take their time about deciding where the gold was hidden. In the meantime they would have to get along without food or water.

But shortly after dawn, a ship sailed into the harbor and anchored close to the *Betsy Anne*. The crew immediately held a meeting in the forecastle, aware that the captain of the newly arrived ship would pay a courtesy call sometime during the morning, as was the custom on the coast. They had little choice as to what could be done. They could tell the visitor that both their captain and mate were sick, but this would be bound to cause suspicion. On the other hand, if they released the two men from the cabin, what was to prevent them from telling the visiting captain that the crew had mutinied and locked them up?

It was decided at last, just as the captain and the second officer of the new ship put off in a dory and were rowed toward the *Betsy Anne*, to release Mr. Sparks but to keep Captain Mulvaney locked up. Sparks, they felt, was the least likely of the two men to cause them trouble.

A knock on the captain's door brought no answer. Nor was there a reply to the second and third knocks. Using his key, Mark Walker opened the door. The cabin looked as if it had been visited by a gale, dishes, bottles, books, charts, an upset table, and broken chairs lying in a heap. Captain Mulvaney lay against one bulwark — dead. Mr. Sparks was crumpled against another — badly injured.

Mark Walker greeted the visitors and told him that both their officers had been sick, but that both were feeling better and that they would return his call the next day. To continue their search for the gold and to make it seem that things were normal aboard ship, the crew divided and went off to the shore.

That night they wrapped Captain Mulvaney in a piece of canvas and rowed him to the island and buried him in a handy cave above the reach of the tide.

Before dawn the next morning the *Betsy Anne* under full sail headed south, but she was seen no more either on the coast or in Nantucket, her home port. Only Mark Walker of all her crew came home, and then as an old man to report that the ship had foundered far away in Malabar Strait in the South Pacific.

We liked his grandson, Sam. He told us many stories of the sea and of the true Garden of Eden, which he said was located on the Indus River. He liked to talk about the

Garden of Eden, which he had seen once, more than about the sea. But I always steered him back, sooner or later, to the story of the *Betsy Anne* and Dead Man's Island.

And always at the end of this story, Sam would take out of his pocket a gold doubloon and pass it around for us to see. It was much heavier than a silver dollar and about the same size, but with six sides. It was a gold doubloon coined in the city of Lima, Peru, in the year 1691, and bore a design of two towers and a dove flying. It was the same Spanish doubloon that Sam's grandfather had taken from the crevice in the leather chest in Captain Mulvaney's cabin.

We used to search Dead Man's Island from the top to the dark caves where the tides came in. Every Saturday when we didn't go to the gravel pit and feast upon cactus apples and ground squirrels, we went there and dug.

We never found a single doubloon or a single sign of Spanish treasure, although we did stumble upon a skeleton washed into a cave, lying there in the dark, loose and bone-white, with empty eye sockets looking out at us. We were sure that it was Captain Mulvaney's skeleton until the police found out and took it away and said that it was a young girl who had drowned in the harbor some months before.

Young Magellans

4

We had planned to leave San Pedro around noon, but noon comes and we find that Rod's bunk is empty and that it has not been slept in. I see now how foolish it was to let him have all of his wages with the city of Los Angeles only twenty miles away.

We hold a short parley and I vote for leaving. The navigator votes to wait until four. Del has discovered some good bottom fishing off the stern of the boat and doesn't care when we leave. We compromise by planning to leave in the middle of the afternoon, which will allow Rod time to get back and still allow us about a five hour run in daylight.

Rod is back sooner than we had expected. He comes scooting up in a water taxi exactly at one o'clock, in time for lunch. He has spent all of his money, so I have to pay the taxi bill. He needs a shave but otherwise looks good. He has a good appetite, too, eating four hamburgers, four dill pickles, a package of potato chips, and a wedge of apple pie topped with a scoop of strawberry ice cream.

During lunch he brings forth a box of chocolates, which he has brought back as a present for the navigator. This gesture makes her feel more kindly toward him, even to the point of asking him if he would like a second piece of pie. But I have plans for Rod when we get under way — a lot of leftover sanding for one thing, and three filters to clean.

We start to bring in the forty-pound Danforth anchor. It is no big task, just a matter of turning on the windlass and watching while it pulls the heavy chain up and through a channel on the prow and drops it length by length into the chain locker. However, when the anchor shank reaches the channel you must turn off the motor, step forward and guide the shank into the channel, taking care to keep your fingers out of the machinery. It is not supposed to work this way. The shank is supposed to come up and fit itself neatly into the channel, without any help. Hopefully, someday we will find a mechanic who can adjust it, along with the alternator and the quacking duck.

In the meantime, I ask Rod to handle this chore. He salutes smartly and says, "Aye, aye, old-timer."

"Old-timer" is something new he has thought up. "And clean off the anchor," I add, pondering on his new name for me, deciding that I don't like it very much. "And when you get through, will you take a look at the filters."

Rod is about to say, "Aye, aye, old-timer," again, but it occurs to him, and rightly, that if he does it I will think up something else for him to do.

We head slowly out of the harbor, giving Rod a chance to wash the anchor thoroughly. It is Sunday and all the Sunday drivers are out, going full bore in every direction, most of them on the wrong side of the buoys.

In the old summer days, when we were not journeying to the gravel pit or digging for doubloons on Dead Man's Island, we went to sea. Each of us chose a log from a great raft of logs that were towed into the harbor from the pine forests of Oregon. The logs were twenty feet long or longer, rough with splinters and streaked with tar. But to us young Magellans, they were proud canoes, fashioned by ax and fire, graceful and fierce-prowed, the equals of any storm.

Each of us straddled a log and in single file, using our

hands, we paddled to the breakwater and sometimes beyond. Hours later, we returned to the harbor and our waiting mothers, the watery world, all the Ocean Seas, encompassed.

The anchor is cleaned and secured. We round the breakwater and head northwest along the high granite cliffs of Point Fermin. When I was a boy the tops of these cliffs were dotted with dozens of piles of abalone shells as high as two-story buildings. The abalones were gathered by Japanese fishermen on the rocks below, the meat taken out and put on wooden trays. The hillside at Palos Verdes was covered with trays of abalone drying in the sun — by the millions.

Sometimes if we hung around long enough the fisherman would give each of us a small abalone. The sun would shrink to a third of its size an abalone that was as big as your hand when it was pried from the rock. You needed a sharp knife to whittle off a sliver that you could put beside your tongue, but you could suck on the sliver all morning, while you went swimming or did anything. For hours it gave off the sweet taste of sea winds and the sea itself.

The dried abalones were packed up and sent off to China, where they brought good prices and were made into soup. There were no laws then, so the fishermen pried abalones off the rocks in all seasons and in all sizes. They stripped the reefs and ledges. Now abalones are protected by law, but they have not come back.

Once there was a vast forest of kelp along this coast. Fishing was good. You could catch a dozen two-pound bass in an hour off Point Fermin or Portuguese Bend. It was good because kelp absorbs the sun's energy, like a tree, and starts a food chain that attracts fish and gives them a place to live.

Then the kelp-cutters moved in and chewed away at the forests. Many of the fish disappeared. Laws were passed to control the cutters and slowly the forest began to grow back. Then the coast had three warm winters in a row — 1957, 1958 and 1959 — and more of the forest disappeared. (The kind of kelp that grows along this shore needs water that is no warmer than fifty-eight degrees.) Then a plague of sea urchins descended. Urchins thrive upon the nutrients that pour into the ocean from the sewers of Los Angeles County. But they like the tender young shoots of kelp plants even better.

A scientist from Caltech and some student volunteers began a campaign against the sea urchins, poisoning and killing them by hand. At the same time they transplanted kelp from Catalina Island to coves along this shore. The transplants have taken hold. Fish are returning.

Farther south, along the coast where we chased the whales around, a different experiment with kelp goes on. Caltech's marine laboratory is raising kelp from the embryo — enough kelp, if all the embryos survive, to fill the Pacific Ocean from rim to rim. The trouble is that with nature handling things only three or four out of 1000 billion do survive.

The embryos come from spores that grow on bottom leaves. A bushel of these leaves is put into chilled water, which is cold enough to squeeze out billions of spores. The spores are placed in tanks where they settle upon fiber-glass cloth. In two or three weeks, if all goes well, these embryos are taken to a site, to the very bottom of the sea, and there scraped off and left to fend for themselves.

Each embryo has two small tails that propel it through the water. But slowly, no faster than three feet an hour. In a couple of days, if it doesn't find a place to fasten to, it dies. One out of every 100,000 embryos does find a place. In nature, only 1 out of 250 billion.

The Caltech lab is having great luck with their kelp raising. In a year or two the coast we have been traveling, from San Diego to San Pedro, will once again be a marine forest. It is now a desert.

Santa Catalina Island is off our port. The island is nineteen miles long and in places two thousand feet high, but we can't see it because it is hidden by a cloud of blue smog. Yesterday when we came into San Pedro the cloud was a yellowish brown. The cloud is sickle-shaped. It runs out from the coast, does a sweep around the island and then curves back toward the land.

We are making nine knots against a light chop as we head away from the eye of the descending sun.

SEVEN

Ship's Log

1

June 5: Arctic Star puts her nose into a stiff westerly and makes the run to Anacapa light in seven hours and ten minutes. She does it without a hitch, without anything or anybody falling overboard, no balky filters, no alternator problems, no stops to reel in fish, large or small.

A new moon shows in the west as we raise Anacapa light. The moon lies on its back with two thin horns raised, meaning, according to the navigator, that it will hold water and that we are in for a spell of wet weather.

Some light is left and I can see the outlines of Anacapa and Santa Cruz Islands. Santa Rosa and San Miguel Islands are hidden. We plan to pass San Miguel, where Juan Rodriguez Cabrillo is buried, when we move on to the north.

These four islands form a loose chain that runs along the coast for about thirty miles. The distance between the coast and the islands varies between ten and fifteen miles, forming the crescent-shaped Santa Barbara Channel, which the Yankee sailors called the Canal. We have entered the Canal and off to starboard lies the town of Ventura, its lights just beginning to blink. A stream flows into the sea here and close by is San Buenaventura Mission, which was built by Father Serra.

We anchor for the night in five fathoms, behind a kelp bed. We would be more comfortable if we went on for two hours more and ducked in behind the breakwater at Santa Barbara. But we want to get an early start for San Miguel in the morning. If we go on to Santa Barbara, we will be waiting for Rod again, as we did at San Pedro. The wind has gone down with the sun. The sea has flattened out, the swells are no more than two feet high and they are coming along at a reasonable pace, so we should be comfortable until morning.

A flock of gray gulls passes over us silently on its way to nest for the night. Shoreward are the lights of the town, a wide river valley timbered with oaks and sycamores. The light is fading but I can make out a spacious beach that ends in a point of land. On this point there was once a large village of round huts. Because of the many canoes owned by the Indians of the village, Cabrillo called it El Pueblo de las Canoas.

Vizcaíno, great namer of California places and renamer of those already named, anchored here in 1602, but did not change its name. He asked his diarist to make a record of their first meeting with the natives.

"A canoe came out to us with two Indian fishermen who had a great quantity of fish. They rowed so swiftly

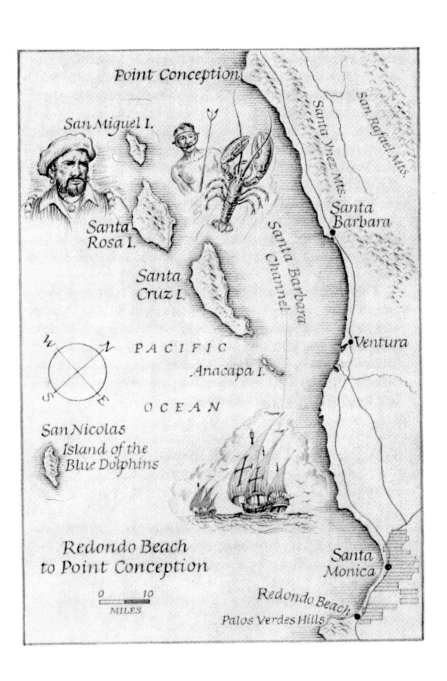

Point Conception

San Miguel I.

Santa Vnez Mts.

San Rafael Mts.

Santa Barbara

Santa Rosa I.

Santa Cruz I.

Santa Barbara Channel

N

PACIFIC

Anacapa I.

Ventura

W   E

S

OCEAN

San Nicolas
Island of the
Blue Dolphins

Redondo Beach
to Point Conception

Santa Monica

0   10
MILES

Redondo Beach

Palos Verdes Hills

that they seemed to fly," the diarist wrote. "After they had gone, five Indians came in another canoe, so well constructed that since Noah's ark a finer and lighter vessel has not been seen."

The village has gone but one of the canoes still exists. It has graceful lines from stern to prow, sweeping curves that give you a feeling of flight and swiftness, even though the canoe sits upon a museum floor. It has not been dug out of the trunk of a tree, but put together with timbers lovingly worked and cleverly bound with sinew and a tarlike caulking. The most striking thing about it is the color, which is halfway between Chinese and fire engine red.

The Chumash Indians, inhabitants of Canoe Town, which they called Xucu, made voyages to the nearby islands in their beautiful canoes. They were a gentle people, who wove pots and jars of a fine and lasting texture from river reeds. They lived in peace with their neighbors, worshiped their gods with thoughtful devotion, and did not last long when the white men came.

The Green Monster

2

Up before dawn and away as the sun rises. In that time Del catches six calico bass by casting into the kelp bed. He fillets them and we have fried bass on our way to San Miguel.

San Miguel Island lies in a zone that the Navy uses for

a bombing range. We are taking a chance of getting a bomb down our smoke stack.

The sea is calm and in two hours we make Prince Island, the tip of a mountain peak at the eastern end of Cuyler Harbor. Above the cove I see through the glasses a small stone cross that is said to mark the grave of Juan Cabrillo. It stands on a treeless and windswept mesa. It looks lonely even in the fresh morning light.

Cabrillo discovered San Miguel by accident. He was sailing north with his two caravels when he ran into a fierce storm while rounding Point Conception, about twenty-three miles to the north. The storm blew his ships straight south to the shores of San Miguel.

His narrator wrote, ". . . there is a good port [Cuyler Harbor] and there are people."

In this port, where we are now anchored, while he rested from his encounter with the storm and made repairs on his ships, Cabrillo fell and broke his shoulder. It was a severe injury, but the "Little Goat" chose to continue his voyage.

He sailed as far north as Fort Ross above San Francisco Bay. In great pain from blood poisoning which had set in, he turned around and sailed back to San Miguel and died there on the third day of January, 1543. His last act was to give his command into the hands of a Levantine, Bartolome Ferrer.

Ferrer sailed north again and reached the coast of southern Oregon. Soon after the start of his return voyage, a storm separated the two caravels. Ferrer, aboard the *San Salvador,* was certain that *La Vitoria* had foundered, but *La Vitoria* finally showed up, nearly a thousand miles to the south, off the coast of Baja California. Her survival was due to the help of the Virgin Mother, so the crew said, and took a mighty vow at the height of the storm to attend church stark naked, should they live. Which they did, being men of their word.

Scurvy-ridden and almost helpless, they arrived in Mexico and were greeted with indifference. They had done nothing so spectacular as Coronado's expedition into the Southwest. Nor had they discovered the long-sought Northwest Passage. Their voyage was duly set down on the royal maps, but its value would have to wait until after Vizcaíno made his voyage many years later in 1602.

We go ashore and climb the bluff and put a scraggly bouquet, which we collect on the way, beside the stone that marks Juan Cabrillo's grave.

The radio has been turned on since we approached San Miguel and I have listened for a Navy broadcast warning us to leave. Now and then I take a look at the horizon, half-expecting to see a Coast Guard boat bearing down upon us. In midmorning we head for Santa Rosa, an island not in the restricted zone.

Santa Rosa was discovered by the "Little Goat" at the same time he discovered San Miguel. It is only a few miles away but much more hospitable, with more places to anchor and many good springs. However, the wind blows equally strong here and wide kelp beds make caution necessary. It is not a good idea to follow fishing boats through the beds in search of fish or an anchorage, for their propellers are usually equipped with special blades to cut the kelp and yours may not be.

Bones of pigmy elephants have been found here, hinting that the island was once a part of the California mainland.

We hunt out a pleasant cove, and in the dinghy go exploring along the shore. We flush two red foxes, and five wild pigs that go crashing away, squealing through the underbrush. Rod has his diving gear on and we leave him off on a shelf of rock, with a spear and a tire iron and his promise that he will bring us a bag of abalones for dinner.

Around noon as we are in the dinghy heading back to the boat, I hear an echoing noise. At first I think it comes from a herd of sea lions fishing in the kelp, but the noise is repeated and Del thinks it is Rod shouting to us. We have been rowing, but I flip on the outboard and we head for the ledge where we left him. It is around a bend and we come upon him suddenly, waving his arms and shouting for us to hurry.

I bring the dinghy into the ledge on a side protected from the surge that is coming in and throw a line and light anchor onto the ledge. I have never seen Rod excited before. He is on his knees, peering down at something in the water. He continues to peer.

"What is it?" I shout.

"Man, I don't know," he shouts back.

"What's it look like?"

"It could be a Moray eel."

"An octopus?" I kid him.

"No."

"How about a sea serpent?" I say, still kidding.

"It's green," he says. "Green and yellow. And, man, is it ever big."

I see nothing in the water so I climb out of the dinghy

onto the ledge and step up back of him where he is kneeling. He points and I stoop down and squint, following the direction of his finger.

"You see the cave there?" he says.

"I see two of them. One just under the surface. One to the right and deeper."

"It's the deep one to the right."

The cave to the right is about four feet under the surface and about ten feet from the bottom. It is about three feet high and of the same width, shaped like a mouth with drooping lips.

"What's the problem?" Del asks.

"The problem is that I want to get whatever is in there," Rod says. "But I'm afraid if I try to go in the cave, he'll spook and come out."

"It may be a big grouper," Del the fisherman says.

"How about floating a bait into the cave?"

"He's no grouper."

"Whatever he is," Del says, "he has to eat. So he may take a bait."

Rod shakes his head. It is clear that he wants to come to grips with the thing in the cave, hand to claw, hand to teeth, and with the spear.

He kneels there on the ledge, looking down into the water. I squint over his shoulder. The water is clear and there is a slight current around the mouth of the cave.

"The tide is falling," I remind him. "The cave will be easier to reach within an hour."

"He'll come out before then," Rod says, and stands up, gripping the spear. "I've got it figured out."

He explains his plan and we gather around to carry it

out. He is to go into the cave, that is settled. He thinks the cave is eight to ten feet deep. He thinks that he will have enough room to wield the spear. As he goes into the cave, at the very same moment, we will block the entrance.

There is a short discussion about how best to do this. Then Rod decides that he needs a light, which he has left on the boat. Del fetches the light, while Rod slips into the water and keeps guard with his spear at the entrance of the cave.

All is ready. The dinghy is in position, just above the cave. The navigator is at the oars. Del and I have two scoop nets that will fit against the mouth of the cave. Each of them being two and a half feet wide, they are more than ample to cover it. Crouching, we wait for Rod to move into the cave.

He adjusts his goggles, turns on the light and sends a beam into the cave. He has the shaft of the spear under his arm. He holds it in one hand, cocked to make a sharp thrust. A current moves him away from the cave a few feet, but he recovers and swims back.

I glance at Del. Our eyes meet and I see that he is thinking the same thing that I am thinking. In a flash, in less than the time that it takes Rod to swim back to the mouth of the cave, I wonder if we are not holding the bag on a snipe hunt. Rod likes practical jokes and what could be funnier than an underwater snipe hunt — with us holding the bag.

As I grit my teeth at the thought, Rod slips into the cave and disappears. I am prepared for him to come popping out with a perch impaled on his spear. I have an answer waiting for him when he holds it up and grins. Let him come.

But Del and I lean over the stern of the dinghy and hold the nets hard against the mouth of the cave. There is no movement below, no pressure on the nets.

"What do you think?" Del asks.

"I think we're chumps," the navigator says.

Still we wait, Del and I straining to hold the nets in place, the navigator to keep the stern of the boat lined up with the cave, all of us staring down into the clear water, waiting for something to happen, for the end to the joke, feeling silly.

I think of the next moment as a horrendous sound bursting from the sea. But they tell me that there was no sound at all. It was an explosion of water from out the cave, as if the whole cave emptied itself at once. The nets flew from our hands. The dinghy canted around against the ledge. The spear rose at an angle from the depths and floated away.

Rod is coming to the surface. He is on the surface. He is struggling with something that he clutches in his arms or something that is clutching him. There is a lot of noise and water flying. I still think that it is the final act of an underwater snipe hunt. A big joke.

Not until Rod, with a great gathering of strength and a triumphant groan, shoves and lifts and pushes his quarry into the boat am I convinced that it is not a joke.

"Man, did I ever sweat," he sputters, clinging to the boat. "I swam in and there he was back in a corner with those black eyes shining in the light and claws waving back and forth. Man, what a sight! I took a lunge at him with the spear and missed. I lost the spear. Then I took after him with my hands."

He stops talking and looks at his hands. They are pretty well cut up. He leans over the gunwale and puts his head down, breathing hard.

The navigator has already left the boat. She is swimming toward the ledge with all her clothes on. Del and I are alone in the boat, facing the largest lobster I have ever seen, probably the largest anyone has ever seen. It has feelers a yard and a half long, pointed claws a yard long, black eyes as big as marbles on four inch stalks, a tail twice as long as your arm and bigger than your leg, a monster armored in a shell of green concrete.

Truthfully, there are no true lobsters in Southern California, only a distant cousin called a spiny lobster. But this lobster is huge. It weighs forty-one pounds and eight ounces. It must be a world's record catch for a spiny lobster.

But Rod can't prove his claim, for we eat the proof that night for supper, in cocktails the next day, and in soup on the three days following and freeze the rest.

Fandango!

3

We had planned to go straight north to Monterey, skipping Santa Barbara until our return trip, but Rod's hands are giving him pain. Instead, we leave early the next day, cross the Canal on a windless morning, and anchor behind the town's breakwater. In Richard Dana's time there was no harbor at Santa Barbara. Ships moored in the open roadstead with slip lines on the anchor, ready to leave within minutes in case of a storm.

Rod gives three blasts on the air horn and a water taxi speeds out to pick him up. He is glad to go ashore, though he tries to hide his pleasure. I don't expect to see him the rest of the day. Santa Barbara is not a port like San Pedro or San Diego, but it is lively.

In the days of the Spaniards, colored tents large enough to handle three hundred people, were raised. No invitations were sent out, but everyone was expected to come. The fandangos lasted all night and often went on for days, the dancers stopping from time to time to take a nap. Musicians from the Yankee ships helped out and once an all-black band of six pieces — a *bombo*, two *tambores*, a timbal and two clarinets — came ashore and played. The Californians were used to waltzes and jotas. They didn't know what to make of the music the band played.

The Spaniards held fiestas, too. A lot of them — whenever they could find an excuse. They dug pits and barbecued two or three steers at a time. They rounded up their best horses and held races. They chased young bulls and threw them to the ground by twisting their tails. They buried roosters in the sand, all except the heads, then raced past on their fast horses and plucked the heads off. They were the best horsemen in the world and knew it. A good saddle could cost a thousand dollars.

Santa Barbara was noted for its beautiful women. One of the most beautiful was Trindad Ortega. A faded old daguerreotype shows her seated, her dark hair gracefully parted, her eyes deep-set and wide, her chin with just a hint of a dimple. She was called "Springtime" by her admirers and Spring Street, one of the principal streets in Los Angeles, was named in her memory.

EIGHT

Trouble

1

E VERY GOOD SAILOR has heard of Point Conception. Dana called it the Cape Horn of California, where it begins to blow the first of January and blows all the year round. I have heard about Point Conception, too.

An hour before dawn of the second morning of our stay in Santa Barbara, having just gathered Rod Lambert into the fold, we head out of the harbor. There is no way to outwit this bleak headland that stands guard at the northern end of the Canal, but we hope that we can lessen the trouble by getting an early start.

At nine o'clock we are two miles off the point, too early for the northwesterlies that blow south of here and begin before noon. But the winds of Point Conception are already here, waiting for us. They greet us from several angles, or so it seems. By the reading the anemometer sends down from the masthead, we see that they

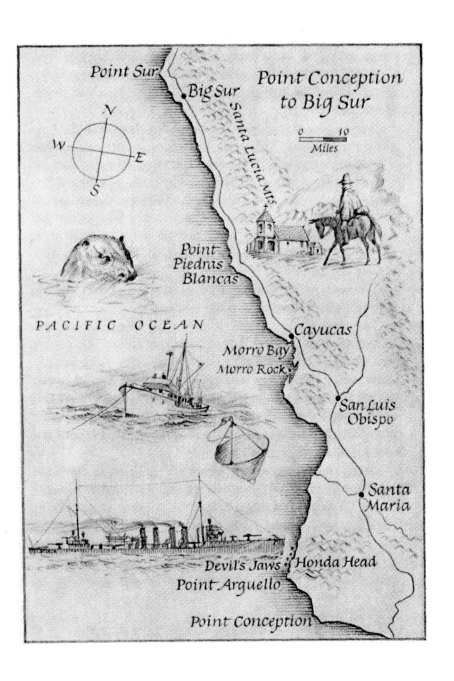

Point Sur

Big Sur

Point Conception
to Big Sur

N

W   E

S

Santa Lucia Mts.

0   10
Miles

Point
Piedras
Blancas

PACIFIC OCEAN

Cayucas

Morro Bay
Morro Rock

San Luis
Obispo

Santa
Maria

Devil's Jaws   Honda Head
Point Arguello

Point Conception

are blowing at twenty-one knots. They feel heavier than that, and with white breakers close off our starboard we move farther out to sea. Danger lies close in, close to the shore, as a rule.

Slanting out away from the shore, the motion of the ship eases and we take less spray over the bow. *Arctic Star* has a deep keel and she is fitted with rollers, fins that run for eighteen feet along each side of the boat, just below the water line. These fins serve as stabilizers, thus slowing down the rocking motion of the boat. But when we straighten out and steer north, we get a lot of movement again, for the seas now are coming at us from the side instead of head on.

We have gone about five miles in this weather and are still off Point Conception when it happens.

The same thing happens at sea with a boat as happens on the land with a car. One minute everything is working fine and the next minute the motor quits. But there is a big difference between the land and the sea. On land you can put on the brake and stop. At sea there are no brakes and even though the engine quits, the boat continues to move with the wind and current, backward or sideways, onto the rocks if there are any around.

There is nothing wrong with the engine. It is the same type that is used in thousands of fishing trawlers up and down the coast from San Diego to Alaska, especially in Alaska where fishermen need an engine that will run in stormy seas night and day without trouble. But you do have to keep the oil clean, and that is our trouble now. The heavy motion of the boat has stirred up sediment in the bottom of the fuel tanks and this has clogged the fuel line.

The engine room of a small boat is always cramped. It is not like your garage at home where you can move around, put things on the floor, and throw out your chest and take a deep breath if you want to. It is cramped and it is hot, machinery you touch is hot and the air you breathe is hot and everything smells of oil. Above all, the engine of a small boat at sea is forever in motion.

When you are stopped dead in a heavy sea, as we are now, it is no place for someone with a weak stomach. This morning Rod Lambert has one, acquired in Santa Barbara. His hands are in bad shape, too, from his encounter with the monster spiny lobster.

As a result, the navigator stands at the helm — in the old days in a storm they used to lash the helmsman to the wheel to keep him from being washed overboard — while Del and I must go below to wrestle with the filters. Before we go I take a look around, at the white breakers and the rocks we are drifting toward. They are about four miles away, so at the rate we are drifting I figure that we have a half-hour to get the engine running.

The boat has slewed around broadside to the waves, so it has a horrendous movement. It is rolling from beam-end to beam-end, and pitching. Chairs and tables have been lashed down in the cabins, but everything is straining to get free, to fly around like birds.

"How about a sea anchor?" the navigator says.

She is beginning to feel the movement of the boat. We all are.

"Where is it?" I ask.

"In the stern, portside locker, unless you put it somewhere else."

I stagger out and along the deck; followed by Del, a good man to have aboard at any time but especially a time like this. I have not put the sea anchor anywhere and it is in the portside locker, where the navigator said it was, but it is filled with fishing gear. I toss the gear on deck, then step into it — a nest of hooks and sinkers, and uncoil the line. Del secures one end of the line to a cleat and tosses the anchor into the sea. A few dozen fishhooks go with it.

A sea anchor is made of canvas. It is about the size of a small umbrella and looks a little like a parachute. It is also called a drag, and this is what it does — it drags along and by its hold upon the water keeps the boat headed into the sea. It is a simple and wonderful device.

Instead of bobbing sidewise *Arctic Star* now straightens up and faces the waves. We go below, Del bumping his head on a beam. We find the wrenches we will need, brace ourselves against fuel tanks and engine, unfasten the fuel lines, and blow them out. We change the filter, which is some ten times the size of a car filter, and put in a new one.

There is another way to do all this, to prevent the filters and fuel lines from clogging and the engine from stopping. You open the pet cocks on the fuel tanks and let the sludge flow into the bilge. Then you turn on the bilge pump and pump the sludge into the sea. This method is quick and foolproof. Many boat captains and especially the captains of big ships use it. Likely as not, you have seen this sludge when it has washed up on the beach.

Everything is fastened together, but we check it again to be sure, knowing, of course, that there is a good chance, even if it is a small one, that the engine will not start. We go above and find the navigator, feet braced and grim, clinging to the wheel. Her job is no fun. Del takes the wheel and I press the starter button. *Who-o-o-o-osh.* She goes! She goes! I rev her up to a thousand and let her idle, then go out and take in the sea anchor.

As I make my way back to the cabin, I glance at the coast. It is close, too close. I put the engine in gear and we gratefully leave the cliffs and line of white breakers astern. The sea is dangerous. It is dangerous at all times and in all weathers. Without warning, it can bring disaster to even the finest ship and the finest captain. The sea is not a place to fool around, to make errors, to be careless.

The Jaws of the Devil

2

Point Conception lies twelve miles astern and we are passing Point Arguello. The wind has lessened. The sea is no longer confused. The waves begin to flatten out, coming toward us now in steady surges.

Three miles north of Arguello stands Honda Head. It is a steep volcanic cliff that rises to a barren mesa. Below the cliff is a sweeping half-circle of rocks and reefs and pinnacles washed by a heavy surf. The Spaniards, returning from the Philippines in their deep-laden galleons, called it *La Quijada del Diablo*, The Jaws of the Devil.

Here, on the eighth of September in 1923, there took place the worst peacetime disaster in the history of the United States Navy. The disaster wrecked seven fine ships in the hands of seven fine captains. It was caused by carelessness.

The seven ships had left San Francisco that morning, with other ships of the fleet, on a speed run to San Diego. All of them were powerful destroyers, more than three hundred feet in length, trim and fast and the pride of the Navy. Their men liked to call themselves the Cavalry of the Sea.

At dusk that night they were racing south at twenty knots, which is twenty-three miles an hour on land. The *Delphy* was in the lead. Behind her steamed the *E. P. Lee*. Then came the *Young* and eleven other destroyers, all in line, one after the other, trying to keep up the set speed of twenty knots and the set distance between ships of one hundred and seventy-four yards.

It was 6:10 by the clock in the chartroom of the flag-ship, *Delphy*, when Captain Watson, Lieutenant Commander Hunter, and Lieutenant Blodgett first began to wonder about their position. In other words, they wondered where they were. They had passed Big Sur ten minutes before and at a close distance of four miles, but had not sighted it because of haze. If they had been able to sight it, then they would have known exactly where they were, for the chart was in front of them and Big Sur was on it.

"The wind and sea are pushing us along," Captain Watson said, "and we have some help from the Japan Current."

"Right, sir," Hunter said, "which should take care of any speed we have lost due to foul bottoms, bad steering, racing screws, currents, and such matters."

The first thing you noticed about "Dolly" Hunter was his eyes. They were a dark, glowing brown, and if they had belonged to a woman you would say that they were beautiful. He was sure of himself, but not overbearing, and he liked to laugh. (His shock of black hair would turn white before the year was out.) He was one of the best navigators in the Navy, with many years of experience at sea and two years of teaching navigation at Annapolis. He did not trust radio bearings — the position of a ship taken from a direction-finder station, such as the station at Point Arguello.

"You can't be sure of them," he said to Captain Watson and Lieutenant Blodgett. "They make a lot of odd errors."

In the midst of their conversation news came over the tube. "Three hundred twenty true at eighteen fifteen," the voice from the radio room said.

Blodgett laid down the new bearing on the chart. "It looks pretty good," he said.

Watson and Hunter studied the new position given them by the Arguello station. Hunter thought that three hundred twenty degrees was fairly close to where they were, but he still did not trust it. Watson said he wished he had a depth finder such as the English Navy used. It was awfully cheap of the United States not to furnish its ships with these new gadgets that told at a glance how deep the water was. Hunter agreed.

"There's no point in slowing down," Watson said. "It's probably three hundred fathoms here. We would never reach bottom."

"If we stop," Hunter added, "we'll spoil our speed run."

Hunter was right, the speed run would be washed out. The *Delphy* would have to slow down to five knots. All the ships in the squadron would have to slow down. It took time to do this. Watson was right, too. The water was probably three hundred fathoms deep and the lead would never reach the bottom.

Furthermore, the report from Arguello had come in at 1815 — 6: 15 P.M. — which meant that they had an hour and forty-five minutes to reach a decision. Not until nine o'clock, Hunter figured, would he have to make the left turn into Santa Barbara Channel. There was plenty of time.

On the other ships of the squadron all was not so serene. There were some who thought that it would be wise not to enter Santa Barbara Channel at all, but to take a course to the right, to the west and on the outside of the channel, thus steering clear of both Arguello and San Miguel. Some thought that they should stop and take soundings. If Arguello were dead ahead, in front of them, the squadron was in twenty to thirty fathoms of water. If they were to the right, to the west of the Arguello lighthouse, then they were in fifty to sixty fathoms.

There was a lot of talk in the chart rooms but nothing was done. Tradition said that you followed the leader.

The leader was Commander Donald Hunter, one of the best navigators in the United States Navy.

The haze grew heavier. You could see no farther than a mile. Following seas made the ships hard to steer, yet they kept in line, plunging through the night at twenty-three miles an hour. The dead-reckoning position plotted on the chart by Lieutenant Blodgett for 8:30 P.M. showed the *Delphy* well to the south of Arguello.

"The bearings we get from Point Arguello put us to the north," he said to Captain Watson, hinting that they should stop and measure the depth of the water.

Watson repeated what he had said before, that the water was too deep to cast a lead, that a stop would spoil their speed run. Donald Hunter agreed.

"Perhaps the visibility will get better," Watson said. "We may be able to see the light at Point Conception."

He paused and glanced at Hunter. Hunter said nothing. He had already spoken. It was his firm belief and he had said so several times in the last hour, that they must change their course at nine o'clock. If they did not change it, if they kept on after the hour of nine in the same direction, then the squadron would run on the rocks at San Miguel Island.

Watson glanced at the chart, at the spot where Blodgett had placed a pencil mark. It was far to the north of Point Arguello, as far to the north as Hunter thought they were to the south. Both positions could not be right. The squadron could not be in two places at once.

Hunter was more apt to be right than Blodgett, who had much less experience. Captain Watson weighed one man against the other, one decision against the other, and after a few moments made up his mind.

"At twenty-one hundred," he said, "change course to ninety-five degrees . . . "

This was a command. It went to the helmsman of the flagship, *Delphy*. It went to all the captains in the squadron, to all the ships speeding along behind them. "At twenty-one hundred — nine o'clock — change course . . ."

The command that Captain Watson gave was wrong. It was disastrously wrong.

The quartermaster left the chart room and went out to the bridge, hoping to catch a glimmer from the Arguello Lighthouse or a sound from its diaphone. He came back to the chart room and waited. He went out to the bridge again and waited, peering into the darkness. He saw no light from Point Arguello. He heard no sound from its horn. He was uneasy.

The bridge of the *Delphy* was dark except for the green glow of the binnacle light. Seven men stood at their stations — the steersman, the quartermaster, the messenger, the signalman, two lookouts, one on the port side of the bridge, one on the starboard, and the Officer of the Deck. Silent, the seven men glanced at the red sweep hand on the ship's clock. They waited and watched for the hour of nine and said nothing.

Captain Hunter checked the new figures that Blodgett had put down on the chart, the new course that Captain Watson had asked for, the course that would take them safely into Santa Barbara Channel — clear of both Point

Arguello and San Miguel Island. The men left the chart room and made their way to the bridge. There Blodgett passed the change-of-course order to the deck officer and told him to signal the turn to the other ships and to sound two blasts on the *Delphy's* whistle exactly on the stroke of nine.

At the hour of nine the two blasts sounded, the rudder on the *Delphy* was put over, the ship swung cleanly to the left in a sweeping curve. Captain Hunter crossed to the port wing of the bridge and looked out. The night was overcast but he could see the lights of the ships that were following.

He watched while each of them swung to the left and fell in behind, about two hundred fifty yards apart. He could just make out the lights of the eighth ship in line, the *Percival.* This meant that visibility was about a mile. He was certain now that Point Arguello lay safely to the north, that by making the turn to the east at the proper time they had missed crashing head on into San Miguel Island and the surrounding reefs.

The ships kept to their speed of twenty-three miles an hour. Their powerful turbines rumbled as they buried their noses in the heavy ground swells. The night was very dark with a haze and no stars. They ran a full five minutes straight toward the east. Then, running out of the haze, they suddenly plunged into a wall of blinding fog.

Hunter had been in fog before. He was famous for bringing ships into port when he could not see his hand in front of him. The truth was, however, that he could see no farther through the fog than anyone else with good eyesight. He was daring and he was lucky and he was skillful. But he could not see through a wall of fog. If he had been able to, then he would have seen in front of him, less than a quarter of a mile away, a mountainous cliff.

The sound that came to him as he stood there on the bridge of the *Delphy* was not made by the turbines nor by her sharp prow cutting through the waves. It was a rasping sound, swift and low-pitched, the sound that a ship's bottom makes when it strikes gravel.

The rasping sound faded quickly. It was followed by a bump, a series of bumps that ended in a violent crash. The crash knocked the nine men who were gathered on the bridge off their feet and against the forward bulkhead.

Commander Hunter pulled himself up and looked out through the fogged glass. To port and straight ahead he saw nothing, but off to starboard and close, he caught a glimpse of a towering rock. The rock, he was certain, was on the shore of San Miguel Island or a nearby reef. The *Delphy* had come too far south before making its eastward turn.

Hunter put his mouth to the speaking tube and shouted a signal to the squadron, "Keep clear to westward, nine turn! Keep repeating. Keep repeating." In Navy code, "nine turn" commanded the rest of the ships to make a ninety - degree turn to the left, all of them moving at once. By this maneuver he hoped to steer them into the safe waters of Santa Barbara Channel.

But the *Delphy* was not aground on the rocks of San Miguel Island, as Commander Hunter thought. She had crashed into the steep red cliffs of Honda Head, into the Jaws of the Devil, twenty-three miles to the north of San Miguel — and three miles north of Point Arguello.

Hunter's command, "Keep clear to westward," was heard by every destroyer in the squadron. Every captain knew the command and tried to take action. But for the six ships racing along at the *Delphy's* stern there was no time — no more than a few seconds — and that was not time enough.

In a great grinding of steel against steel and steel against rock, while sirens screamed and searchlights darted crazily across the sky, one after the other in tight formation the six destroyers followed the Delphy into the Devil's Jaws.

Gray dawn found them where they crashed, strewn across reefs and impaled upon rocks, half-awash and pounded by heavy seas. Twenty-three men were killed.

Years later, after he had left the Navy, I met Donald Hunter and we began a friendship that lasted until his death. He sometimes talked to me about the disaster at Honda Head. Kneeling on the floor he would spread out the chart and point to Arguello and San Miguel and show me how and why the seven fine ships went on the rocks. I heard the story many times, much as I have told it here. It was always the same story. But nothing, not the naval inquiry, the testimony of other officers, nor the location of the wrecked ships, ever convinced Dolly Hunter that the signals from Point Arguello were accurate.

Sea Otter

3

The coast makes a bend to the right after it leaves

Arguello and the Devil's Jaw, curving in toward Morro Bay where, if all goes well in the engine room, we will anchor for the night.

Off to our left the sun is setting. It looks much larger than it does overhead. It begins to flatten on the underside as it touches the horizon, then spreads out and seems to melt into the sea.

We are moving along at half speed, just outside a wide field of kelp and about a mile from shore. We are moving at half speed because Del has a line out, trying to catch a big fish for supper. I almost hope he doesn't catch a big fish. Or a small one, either. I am a little tired of fish. Corned beef hash with chili peppers and a couple of eggs on top sound better. Del is trailing a metal lure called a Killer Diller. It bounces crazily along from wave to wave, catching the glow from the sky.

The boat slows down and begins to drift, still with the engine running. I am on the flydeck and see no sign of a fish on Del's line. Then the navigator calls up and says that a band of sea otter are swimming around in the kelp off our starboard bow. There are four of them, at least that is all I can see through the binoculars. In the old days, about the time of Richard Dana, there were thousands of otter along the coast.

The otter are about two hundred yards away. They see us, judging from their actions, then they decide that we are not dangerous and go back to feeding. The water is three fathoms deep along here and they dive together, stay down for less than two minutes and come up together, as if on a signal.

They have something in their mouths and hold it there

until they have turned over and are floating on their backs. They lie with their hind feet spread wide, their doglike front feet resting upon their chests. Whatever it is that they have found on the ocean floor, it is still in their mouths.

We are close to them now, perhaps a hundred yards away, but they accept us. One of them shades its eyes against the sun with its paw so as to get a better look at the boat. The navigator holds our position by using the reverse gear.

I see now that the otter have small clams in their mouths. On each of their furry chests is a rock about the size that you can comfortably hold in your hand. Using this rock as an anvil, the otter takes the clam from his mouth and beats it against the anvil until the shell breaks open.

The rocks they are using as anvils are tools and they handle them like tools. They don't shape the rocks but they do choose them from other, less usable rocks. You wonder what this little animal might do if he had fingers and an opposing thumb as we have, instead of doglike paws.

Otter like to raft — to float on their backs in a group. I have seen them wrap strands of kelp around their stomachs to keep from drifting away on the current. A mother usually gives birth to one baby, seldom more often than one every five years, which she nurses for about eighteen months. She ties kelp around it to keep it safe when she dives for food.

You might think that otter are vain because they spend much of their time stroking themselves as they float around. But the truth is, they could not live otherwise, though their fur is lustrous and dense. Unlike the seal, they lack an underlayer of fat to keep them warm. By grooming themselves they create air pockets in their fur and these pockets keep them from freezing in water that is no colder than fifty-five degrees.

Otter are gentle creatures, gentle with one another, and great lovers of fun. Along with the dolphin they are the most joyous of all the animals in the sea. It is sad that out of the hundreds of thousands that once inhabited our coast from Alaska to San Nicolas--the Island of the Blue Dolphins--the hunters have left us only a handful.

And the hunters will leave us fewer of everything, if only they have their way. For all wild things — everything that creeps or walks or flies, whether clothed in fur or feathers — are their target. All the defenseless creatures along these shores are at the mercy of this backward group that equates slaughter with manhood.

Morro

4

We coast along a curving beach, where a white surf shows in the darkness, and sight the beacon on Morro Rock. The harbor opening is narrow so we take our time, keeping the red buoys close on our starboard. The channel makes a sweeping right turn and at the end of it, finding no place to moor, we turn back and pull in beside some fishing boats lying against a pier.

A man comes on the deck of the nearest boat and I ask him if we can tie up. He is tied up to another boat, which is tied up to another boat that is tied to the pier, which makes us the fourth boat out.

"We're leaving at five," he says.

"So are we," I answer.

"You're welcome," he says.

We put out three bumpers along the side to keep the hulls from scraping, Rod steps aboard the fishing boat, I toss him our lines, and we are snug for the night. Fortunately, because the whole harbor is stacked up this way, gunwale to gunwale.

Morro Bay is the center for red abalone fishing. Red abalone is apt to be sweeter and more tender than the gray and black abalones. All of them are as tough as shoe leather unless they are carefully sliced to the proper thinness, softened by a dozen or more sharp raps with a wooden mallet, but not made too soft, rolled in very fine cracker crumbs, then dropped into a skillet of hot butter or lard and cooked fast — and this is important — for just thirty seconds on each side.

It is a nice surprise when the skipper of the fishing boat we are tied to comes aboard with a pan of abalone, all sliced and pounded. Del started a couple of apple pies when it got too dark for him to fish and these are baking now in the oven. Maybe the fisherman has smelled the pies and this is reason for his generosity.

His name is Bill Sterling. He is single, we learn, and lives on his boat the year round. He is thin-faced but stout in the body and cured a mahogany color by the sun. He is an abalone fisherman, or at least he has been.

"I don't know what I'll be doing this time next year," he says. "Fishing is bad and getting worse."

"Where do you fish?" I ask. "Around here?"

"No, not anymore. Abalone are fished out around here. I go north, about a day's run north, up to Gorda and farther."

I know what his problems are. I have been reading about them.

"You mean fished out by the otter?" I say.

"Where did you hear about otter?"

"From the newspapers."

"What you see in the newspapers is mostly lies." He looks at me suspiciously. "What side you on? Fisherman or otter?"

I am on the side of the sea otter, but I am not going to say so, not right now. I want to hear his story and I may not hear it if he knows where I stand.

He waits for me to answer, rolling a cigarette, pouring the tobacco out of a sack, spilling some on the floor, licking the edges of the brown paper. He waits for me to say which side I am on.

"I like the otter," I finally say. "I haven't seen many of them, only six or eight here and there, playing along the rocks up at Big Sur. I like to watch them."

"If they were taking the bread right out of your mouth, would you still like to watch them?"

"I wonder."

"I don't have anything against otter. They're like dogs, seagoing dogs . . . "

"Like cats, too," I break in. "Their young are called kittens, for that reason, I guess."

"Cats or dogs, it mounts up to the same thing. They're putting us abalone men out of business. You know how much an otter eats?"

I know that they have big appetites, but I shake my head.

"Take a guess?"

"Two abalones a day."

"Guess again."

"Four."

"You'll never guess so I'll let you in on the facts." Sterling's cigarette has gone dead and Rod steps forward and lights it with his big flame thrower. "An otter eats twenty-five percent of his weight every day. If he weighs forty pounds, he eats ten pounds of abalone. At three dollars a pound wholesale, it means that one measly otter eats thirty dollars' worth of abalone every day of his life, or almost eleven thousand dollars' worth every year. And that's wholesale. At retail, at five dollars a pound . . . Well, you figure it out."

"Eighteen thousand, two hundred and fifty dollars," says Rod Lambert, who has a quick mind for figures.

"Almost twenty thousand dollars a year, retail," Sterling says.

He gives me a hard look, the same look he would give an otter if it suddenly appeared. I am getting a look from my wife, too, which is meant to encourage me to say what I really think and not pussyfoot around.

"They eat a lot besides abalone," I say. "Sea urchins, snails, crabs, sea squirts, mussels, tube worms. They also eat the starfish that eat abalone. Starfish probably eat as many abalone as the otter."

Sterling's cigarette again has gone dead and Rod steps forward and lights it. Sterling knows now that he is dealing with the enemy. He draws deep on his cigarette, so deeply that the smoke doesn't appear for half a minute, and then it comes out through his nose.

"We were harvesting over five million tons of abalone just ten years ago," he says, trying to be patient and keep his temper. "Last year we harvested five hundred thousand ton. This year we'll harvest less. Next year, who knows?"

I remember the abalone shells piled as high as two story houses along the slopes of Palos Verdes. "The harvest gets smaller every year," I say, "because the fishermen take too many. The abalones need a chance to grow and propagate."

"We only can take them seven and one half inches and larger. That's the law. There's no law for otter. They claw them off the rocks any size, the size of a nickel if they feel like it."

"What do you want to do?" I ask.

"Get rid of them."

"How?"

"It don't matter how," Bill Sterling says. I think that he would like to kill them, but doesn't want to say so. "Move them out of here, anywhere."

"But this is their home. They've been living here for a thousand years. Five thousand years. Ten thousand years. Maybe longer."

"The trouble with you bleeding hearts is you never think of the guy that has to make a living."

I have been thinking of the guy who has to make a living, but I quit thinking about him when he brings in the "bleeding heart" part.

"What do you mean by bleeding heart?" I ask quietly.

"Someone who is always sticking his nose in someone else's business," Sterling says, also speaking quietly.

"That's not a very good definition," I say. "The otter's business is mine. It should be everyone's business because the otter can't take care of himself. He is helpless. You hit him over the head with a club and he won't fight back. You shoot him and he sinks to the bottom without fuss. You chase him out of his home and he'll live as best he can until he starves."

"It don't matter if a human starves," Sterling says.

"Sure it matters," I say. "But you're a healthy young man and if you don't catch abalone you can catch something else. You are not going to starve. You can go where you want. You can do what you want. You are free and alive."

"Thanks," Sterling says, backing out of the cabin. "Thanks for nothing."

"Won't you have a piece of pie?" the navigator says.

Bill Sterling retreats. He is already out the door. He is on his own boat and he disappears. I hope that sometime during the night he doesn't bore a hole in our good cedar hull, a little round hole below the water line.

But the boat is still afloat the next morning at 5 A.M. and as we untie he waves, and I wave back and thank him for the abalone. Rod, who does the untying, thanks him too — he should, since he ate most of them. There is a lot of diving gear on the stern of Sterling's boat, which

Rod carefully looks over. For a moment I am afraid he is going to jump ship and sign on with Sterling for an abalone hunt, but he finally straggles aboard and we take in our bumpers and shove away.

NINE

The Gray Ox

1

THE CLIFFS we are now running beside are black where the waves break against them, but farther up their sides they are yellow and red. Behind them is the wild Santa Lucia Range that changes color as the morning advances. From time to time we see through the glasses small herds of grazing deer, and close to Big Sur there is a green meadow with a cow and a calf standing in it, high above the sea.

> "Pretty, pretty, indeed,
> Is a dark brown cow
> In a pale green mead."

We have not met Father Serra since we left San Diego, where he founded the first of his missions. Near Monterey, where we will anchor tonight if all goes well, is his second mission. Originally it had been in Monterey itself, and then Serra moved it five miles away to Carmel Valley on a slope overlooking a plain that runs down to a river and the sea. It is called San Carlos Borromeo de Carmelo.

Father Serra tramped up and down this coast and founded many missions, but San Carlos was his favorite. It is the most beautiful of all the missions, possibly because it has been rebuilt seven times since it was built in 1770. When his work was done, when it took little more than a day to travel from one mission to another, all the way from San Diego to San Francisco, Serra came back here to die.

His long life and its meaning may be summed up in two happenings: the first was his forgiveness of the serpent he encountered on the trail from Vera Cruz to Mexico City. The second was an incident that took place at San Carlos Borromeo toward the end of his life.

Serra had bought a mother hen and her brood from a trading ship that stopped in Monterey. He prized these chickens and guarded them with great care because they were the only ones for miles around. His zeal, however, was no match for an Indian woman and her son who stole the coop and cooked the chickens. (California Indians, were sometimes wily thieves, picking up with their bare toes anything that was lying around loose, even while you were talking to them.)

The theft was traced to the woman, who said she had stolen because she was hungry. Serra forgave her. Not long before his death the same woman, now sickly, came to see him. He wanted to give her something valuable,

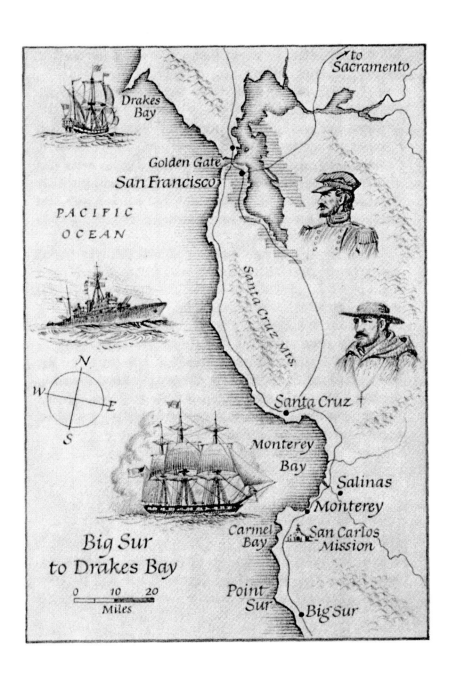

to
Sacramento

Drakes
Bay

Golden Gate
San Francisco

PACIFIC

OCEAN

Santa Cruz Mts.

N

W   E

S

Santa Cruz

Monterey
Bay

Salinas

Monterey

Carmel
Bay

San Carlos
Mission

Big Sur
to Drakes Bay

0   10   20
Miles

Point
Sur

Big Sur

but the only thing he could find was a worn-out blanket, the only covering he had.

Palou, his friend, said, "You are paying her for the chickens, I presume?"

Serra confessed that the theft had been on his mind. "Now it is forgotten," he said.

Serra died on a wooden pallet. Clasped in his arms was a wooden cross that he had brought with him from his home on the island of Majorca and had carried with him always on his wanderings through Mexico and on the trails he traveled in California.

The Gray Ox, as he liked to call himself, was buried beside his friend Father Crespi, according to his wish and in his best robe. He had two robes. One was in tatters and it was kept only to patch the good robe.

There are rumors that Father Serra's tomb is now empty. Sometime soon after his burial, so the story goes, a mysterious Spanish ship anchored at Monterey. In the darkness of night a squad of soldiers and sailors rowed to the beach below the mission, opened the tomb, and carried Father Serra's bones back to the ship, which at once raised anchor and sailed off to Spain.

Monterey

2

We pass Point Pinos and its pines shaped by the wind, Point Lobos, the mouth of the Carmel River, and the rosy towers of San Carlos Borromeo. Sea lions are baying from the rocks, at us I am afraid, but there are no pelicans. This is the time of day that they usually come home from fishing and begin to settle down for the night on the high rocks where they are safe from the tide. I have never been past Lobos without seeing them. I wonder if the poisons that are killing off our pelicans in the south are killing them here, too.

Night comes on clear as we approach the lights of Monterey. The wind smells more of the harbor than of the sea. It is a good smell, nonetheless, made up of kelp, and water that crabs have been boiled in, baskets of shucked clams, and fish, lots of fish.

Monterey was the capital when Spain owned California, later when the Mexicans took it over, and later for a time when the United States took it away from Mexico. The town has had a stormy past but shows no scars. Slow and peaceful, life centers around the harbor, as it did in the old days.

All of the Yankee ships were supposed to stop in Monterey to pay an excise tax to the Mexican government on the goods that they had for sale and to buy a trading license. And some of them did. The ones that did not were called contrabandistas.

A common practice was for one ship to get permission to trade, sell its goods in Monterey or Santa Barbara or San Pedro, then sail off to one of the islands for a rendezvous with a contraband ship. From the hold of the contrabandista the trader got a new stock of untaxed goods, and then continued to trade along the coast. When this stock ran out he rendezvoused again.

The trading ships were actually floating stores, fitted

out amidship from port to starboard bulwarks. Wide counters ran around three sides of the trade room and slab shelves extended from floor to deck beams. Shelves held bolts of calico, muslin, dimity, and silk. Bonnets decorated with knots of French flowers. Lacework, beads, sashes of all colors. The middle shelves were filled with things for the kitchen and table: firkins of salt pork, wine in kegs and stone jugs, tubs of salt, half-chests of tea, cacao, olive oil, flitches of bacon, and a large assortment of spices. Counters were stacked with plain and silver mounted saddles, bridles, fancy headstalls, lengths of iron, hoes and plows, wooden churns and noggins, small pigs of lead, and mold for making bullets. From the timbers overhead hung bunches of tobacco and braided strings of white onions.

It is strange that this unprotected wealth failed to attract a swarm of pirates. But except for Sir Francis Drake, who came along before there were any traders on the coast, only two showed up, both of them at the same time. One was a French pirate, Hippolyte de Bouchard, the other was an Englishman, Peter Corney.

Bouchard was in command of the *Argentine*, a large frigate that mounted forty-five guns. His crew of two hundred and sixty men was the scouring of four continents. Corney was captain of the *Santa Rosa*, with eighteen guns, American officers, and a crew of one hundred, also jailbirds from many lands.

As Corney and Bouchard together sailed into the bay, the citizens of Monterey fled to the surrounding hills. They took with them their livestock and everything of value that they were able to carry. The pirates sent a few shells whizzing over the town and then went ashore and strutted up the main street with flags flying and a band playing a jaunty English tune. They collected a large store of food, enough fine Spanish raiment to clothe their half-naked crews, and sailed south on the prowl for more California loot.

Robert Louis Stevenson must have heard about these freebooters when he lived in Monterey, because he was very interested in California history. But for some reason he did not put them into a story, surely a literary misfortune. How exciting it would be to have a companion to *Treasure Island*! And yet on second thought, perhaps it is just as well that he left Bouchard and Corney alone, to the files of history. They would never have measured up to Long John Silver and his peg leg, to two-fingered, tallow-faced Black Dog, to Bill with a livid white saber cut across one cheek and a great love for the ditty "Fifteen Men on a Dead Man's Chest," or to the eyeless beggar in the tattered cloak.

Odd that Stevenson thought so little of *Treasure Island* that he published the story under a borrowed name, "Captain George North," and, misreading what he had done, burdened it with an uninspired title — *The Sea Cook*. He thought so little of *Treasure Island*, in fact, that he criticized England's prime minister for reading it. The great William Gladstone sat up all night devouring the story and then told his friends about it. Learning of the prime minister's enthusiasm, Stevenson said that instead of reading *Treasure Island*, Gladstone "would do better to attend to the imperial affairs of England."

Lean John Brown

3

Monterey also had a small part in the Mexican War.

After Commodore Stockton had sent his sailors and marines to help the men trapped on Starvation Peak in the Battle of San Pasqual, he fought a successful skirmish at Los Angeles. In high spirits he then sailed off for Monterey.

But he was no sooner in Monterey than a band of three hundred Californians surrounded the small American force he had left in Los Angeles. Outnumbered about six to one, cut off from food and water, forced to make bullets from lead water pipes, the American captain knew that unless he got help his small army would perish, that his only hope was to send a message to Stockton in Monterey. The best horseman in the besieged camp was a farm boy named John Brown. The captain sent for him.

"I understand you're a good horseman," the captain said.

"Some say that, Captain."

"Can you ride to Monterey?"

"If anybody can."

"In how many days?"

"How far is Monterey?"

"About four hundred and sixty miles."

John Brown pondered. He was tall and bony, with a long hollow-cheeked face, and yellow hair that hung to

147

his shoulders. The Californians called him Juan Flaco — Lean John.

"Ought to do it in four days," he said.

The captain stared at him. "No man can ride that fast. You've got to change horses, stop to eat and sleep. Can you make it in twice that time?"

"Four days," Lean John said. "I'll sleep when I get there."

"We'll figure on eight days." The captain took a bundle of cigarette papers from his pocket and gave them to the young soldier. "Hide these somewhere on your person. All of them bear my seal and the words 'Believe the bearer.' You know the bad conditions here. When you reach Monterey give the information to Commodore Stockton. If he isn't there, to anyone in authority."

Lean John tied the cigarette papers in his hair. "When do I set off, Captain?"

"As soon as you can."

John rubbed his chin. "I'm ready about now."

"What do you want to take in the way of arms and provisions? "

"Nothing," said Lean John, "except my spurs."

Lean John rode quietly out of the compound. The dust softened the sound of hoofs. The houses were dark and he saw no one. Beyond the plaza he increased his pace, and after skirting Fort Hill, where a sentry got up out of the brush and challenged him, he gained high ground above the pueblo. The moon had not risen. The trail was dark. He spurred his horse to a trot, heading into the northwest.

He had picked the best horse in the corral. It was a

California horse and understood nothing except Spanish, but it was a stocky animal, with a deep chest and an easy gait that ate up distance. If his luck held he might be able to ride it all the way to Santa Barbara, where it would be easy to get a fresh horse, unless the Spaniards had taken the town. If that had happened he'd have to find another one somewhere. Five or six good horses ought to get him through to Monterey.

He looked up at the sky. He had told the captain that he'd get there in four days. He had said it without thinking very much. Four days had popped into his mind and he had said it right out, without giving it another thought. Four days. He wished now he had said five. Six would be better, counting bad luck he might run into. But he had said four days, so it was up to him to make good.

There was a shine in the east and he guessed it was the moon coming up. One thing, he had been smart enough to stand out against dragging along a rifle, like the captain kept saying he should. What was the good of a rifle if you were jumped by a dozen Californians? It was just extra weight to tote. He hadn't wanted to take anything to eat, either, but the captain had given him an order on that one. It didn't amount to much, just jerky, and moldy at that.

The trail was clearer now, winding through low hills. They reminded him of the hills around Monterey, except that these were covered with brush instead of pine trees. That was sure a pretty town, Monterey, with the hills coming right down to the sea and the sea blue enough to startle a man, and the waves coming in, and birds flying.

The worst thing was that he was going to get lonesome, with no one to talk to, unless he could pick up someone on the way. He couldn't even talk to the horse. A man could get a lot of company from a horse if it understood what you were saying. But there wasn't any pleasure in talking to a Spanish horse.

The low hills were behind him and the country was flattening out. He didn't hear anything, except a coyote far off, and a bear snuffling in the brush, and the sound of his horse breathing steadily. He figured he must be through the enemy lines, but it was funny that he hadn't seen anyone or heard a hoof. He was thinking this when he saw off to his right some shapes moving along a shallow draw. They would likely be cattle, he thought. But the next moment, while he watched, the shapes changed direction and started toward him. He saw that they were men on horses, about fifteen of them.

His horse leaped under the spurs and he swung down on the far side of his saddle, out of sight. A musket ball hit somewhere close, and the crash came an instant later. The horse wheezed, stumbled, and recovered. He straightened in the saddle and held its head up. Something wet was trickling on his leg; he knew then that the horse had been hit, low and back of the saddle, through the belly. He looked over his shoulder and saw the Spaniards about two hundred feet back.

Another musket ball plowed the air to one side of him. They were close now and yelling, but they weren't gaining, in spite of the way his horse had been hit. The moon was up and it shone bright on the trail. He bent over the saddle and hoped the horse would hold out until he could make a dash for a brushy slope he spotted ahead.

He didn't see the ravine, and later when he thought about it, he decided that the horse hadn't either. It was about thirteen or fourteen feet across in the middle of the trail and running at a right angle. He had no chance to set his spurs, but at that moment another shot struck the horse in the back, and it leaped, cleared the ravine, staggered, but kept galloping. He could hear the Spaniards pulling up, shouting and cursing, as he swerved off to his left into the brush.

The horse didn't slow, though it was beginning to breathe hard, and his leg was wet from blood. The brush petered out on the top of a round hill, but he crossed a narrow arroyo and rode into more brush. When that petered out he couldn't hear the Spaniards any longer. All he could hear was the heavy gasps of his horse. He pulled in on the bit, but the horse did not answer. Then, with all feet in the air, it seemed to collapse under him, like a pricked bladder.

The next thing he knew he was lying on the ground. He was skinned up, but in one piece. He got up and went back to the horse. It lay on its side, not even gasping now, its legs all tangled up. He waited for a while. Then he unfastened the *reata* from the saddle, undid the cinches and pulled the saddle off the horse. He stood up and looked around. He figured he was about twenty miles from the nearest American ranch, Las Virgenes.

The saddle got heavy. After about two miles he left it under a tree, pulled off his spurs and put them in his pocket. He took a sight on the North Star and another look at the country. If he walked fast he should get to the ranch by sunup. Monterey seemed far off. He hoped that the next horse would be as good as the last horse.

Two days later, inland from Point Arguello, having ridden almost three hundred miles without sleep, Lean John dropped from his horse and lay down in the grass.

He had no watch but he judged from the Big Dipper that it was about eleven o'clock. Tom Lewis, lying beside him, was already asleep, snoring flat on his back. He had picked up Tom Lewis at Las Virgenes. That was two nights ago when he had walked twenty-seven miles to the ranch house to find another horse. Tom Lewis was a good companion, but Lean John wished that he were stronger, because then they could have ridden on instead of stopping. But he was a good talker and that was important.

Everyone had been helpful along the way. He had given the cigarette papers to three different men — he remembered their names: Lieutenant Talbot at Santa Barbara, Thomas Robbins and Lewis Burton — and they had given him fresh horses. It was funny what a cigarette paper with some words scribbled on it would do.

He thought about Monterey, and the pines growing down to the sea and the girls in bright-colored dresses, but they seemed far away.

He woke up with the Dipper shifted around and the sky black. He must have been asleep for five hours at least. He gave Tom Lewis a shove with his foot and walked to his horse, but when he got in the saddle and looked down Tom was still snoring. He went over and gave him another shove. Tom sat up then, half up on one elbow, and mumbled that he couldn't go on. He was plumb jiggered out.

Lean John, deciding that he wouldn't waste any more time with Tom, lifted himself to the saddle and spurred his horse to a gallop. He showed another one of his papers at dawn and got another fresh horse and galloped away. All day, every time he came across an American, he took a paper out of his hair and traded it for a horse, a good horse too. It was sure funny about those papers. He hoped he would have one left over for a souvenir.

It was black night again when he rode into Monterey, with fog drifting low so he couldn't see the pines or even the sea. The streets were deserted and he didn't see one girl. He felt pretty good riding up to the Customs House, tired and hungry, but when he got down from the saddle his legs wouldn't work. They were bent to the shape of every horse he had ridden in the last three days.

He felt like lying down, but he couldn't until he took off his pants and sloshed cold water on his legs. He felt pretty bad, but the worst thing was that Commodore Stockton was not in Monterey. He was in San Francisco. That was bad news, but anyway he had come through — someone said it was four hundred and sixty miles, but someone else said it was ten miles less. Whichever, it was a long way, a long way to come and not see Commodore Stockton or a girl.

Then he heard them making plans — the mayor and someone else — about sending another rider on to San Francisco. As long as he had made it this far, he wasn't going to sit still for anything like that. The mayor promised to wake him up after three hours, and when he did a fellow by the name of Jacob Dye gave him the loan of his best racehorse.

It was sure a fine horse, the best he had ever seen, and he made good time, riding through the dark. When the sun came up, he was in San Jose. He had trouble getting another horse, so he lost four hours that he didn't want to lose and started off again, swearing he'd go back to Monterey someday soon.

Lean John, having ridden more than five hundred miles in five days, stood on the shore at San Francisco. Commodore Stockton's ship lay at anchor nearby. Lean John waved his hat to catch attention and saw a longboat put off and head toward him. He took the last two cigarette papers from his matted hair. One he would give to the commodore and one he would keep for himself as a souvenir. He had made a good ride, sure enough. The only thing he wished now was that Monterey hadn't been so darned fogged up, so he could have seen a pretty girl or two.

Lean John would have liked Monterey tonight. It is cool and the harbor lights sparkle. There are so many lights that it is hard to find the channel, but we take our time, and choose a place where we have a little room to swing at anchor.

He would have liked the town in the morning, too, and the black-haired girls in bright colors going down to work and the boats unloading fish caught during the night. And other boats like them — trim and high-prowed, the ones that can take a beating from the sea and still come home, which are known everywhere on the coast by the name Monterey — the little boats that are refueled, given supplies, and washed down, preened for evening, when they will slip quietly out of the harbor, like so many birds, to fish again.

They used to go seining for sardines, these sturdy Montereys, but the silvery little fish has long since disappeared. A haul of five thousand tons in a single night once was common. It is no longer. The sardine has gone.

Message

4

The navigator and I go ashore to buy fresh vegetables and check at the post office for mail. There are no bills, not a bill from anybody, one advantage of going to sea. But we do have a letter from the man in San Diego who sold us our boat. Reading its alarming contents, I am surprised that he hadn't tried to get in touch with us by ship-to-shore telephone.

The letter reads:

> I have just learned through reliable sources that Rod Lambert has a bad reputation among people he has worked for. Smith over at the Smith Boat Works tells me that he is working on a boat that the owner brought in with a hole punched in the bow, put there by Lambert. Jim Bishop at Marine Products also gave me some bad news. Lambert brought a forty-five-footer up from Mazatlan last March and burned out the refrigeration and one motor — to the tune of ninety-seven hundred dollars in repairs. I hardly know what to suggest in the situation, but thought you should know . . .

I look at the navigator and she looks at me. Neither of us is surprised.

"What do you want to do?" I say.

"There's not much to do," she answers. "We have to have somebody to help out."

The reason we do, now more than ever, is that Del is down with ear trouble. It is something that affects the inner ear. It acts like seasickness. It came on him shortly after we broke down off Point Conception and I kidded him about being seasick until I learned that it was something else. I urged him to come ashore with us this morning to see a doctor, but he is scared of doctors and would rather suffer, like most of us.

"What I am afraid of," I say, "is that Rod will take a notion to go fishing for abalones or something while we're ashore."

"Del is on board."

"Sure, but he's in his bunk sicker than a dog."

We go to the store and buy a basket of vegetables. The buying goes on for a long time because the vegetables are very fresh, the finest the navigator has ever seen. She asks the clerk where they come from and he says that they come from across the mountains in the Salinas Valley. And she asks him where that is and he tells her exactly where Salinas Valley is, near what city and so forth.

During this long encounter I am in a stew about being away from the boat. I am beside myself. I read the letter over again. I seem to remember that I heard the story of a cruiser being taken to Catalina without the owner's permission, run on a rock, a hole put in the hull, the hull patched up so the owner wouldn't know. And the owner didn't know until one day in a heavy wind the boat sprang a leak. I remember the story now, but of course it never occurred to me that Rod Lambert was the one mixed up in it.

We are unable to find a taxi and it is a long walk back to the wharf with all the Salinas vegetables. I walk fast, worrying all the way about the boat.

"We should have asked Rod for a reference," I say. "We just took his word for everything. Sort of stupid, don't you think?"

"Yes," says the navigator, sweetly.

This doesn't help to allay my fears. I see the boat leaving the harbor. Del is locked in his cabin, too sick to care what is happening.

We walk along in silence. I wonder why it is that the navigator, who is so smart about everything else, wasn't smart enough to tell at first glance that Rod Lambert was a bad risk.

I see the boat speeding north, smoke pouring out the stack, the engine straining, spray flying.

Then we come to a place where I can look down at the bay. A great surge of relief! The *Arctic Star* has gone neither north nor south. She lies serenely at anchor among a flock of fishermen, just where we left her, and Rod is on the stern reading a magazine. There's work he should be doing, but who cares? I am overjoyed that she is safe!

TEN

San Francisco

1

SIR FRANCIS DRAKE missed the Bay of San Francisco, sailing blithely by it on a summer's day, which is very easy to do. Bartolome Ferrer, Cabrillo's brave lieutenant, also sailed past as did many of the early sailors. When the bay was discovered at last, it was not from a ship but from the back of a horse.

Two weeks after Gaspar de Portola came into California with Father Serra, he struck out for the port of Monterey, which had been sighted from the sea. He took with him a party of sixty-four soldiers, muleteers and Indians, as well as eight Catalan volunteers who carried axes to open a passage through the heavy forests that were expected. Portola didn't find Monterey or forests, but to his great surprise stumbled upon the magnificent Bay of San Francisco.

Without radar we too would have missed San Francisco as we plow northward into a heavy swell, the air dusty and a heavy haze piled up at the entrance. Following the scene that shows on the radar, we keep well over to the right, in the slow lane, so to speak, and make our turn to the east close to Seal Rocks — close enough to hear the seals barking. Danger lies to port, off to the left where ships are moving in and out of the bay.

Golden Gate Bridge looms high above us, swinging out into space from its vast abutments. The great cables that carry it from shore to shore hang like spider webs in the wet haze. Once past the bridge we can see much better. By sight we thread our way through a stream of ships and barges and small boats, and find shelter at Sausalito before dark.

Rod has been quiet since his encounter with the forty-one-pound lobster, but now his wounds are healed, and before the anchor is settled he stands on deck, bag in hand. He bought himself a fisherman's knitted cap in Monterey and his shirt has been freshly washed and mended.

This is Sunday afternoon and I tell him as he steps into the dinghy that we plan to leave early Tuesday morning. "Be sure to be on board sometime Monday night," I say.

"Man, you wouldn't leave without me," he answers.

"We're leaving Tuesday morning," I caution him, "with or without."

"Aye, aye, Ratso," he says.

He has given up calling me "Captain," and for the last couple of days has been using this new name.

Rod is handsome in his checked trousers and his new fisherman's cap and his clean shirt that the navigator spent an hour mending and pressing. Maybe one of these days the navigator will sew on the two buttons that are missing from old Ratso's yellow windbreaker.

Del starts the outboard motor — it's perhaps the only outboard motor in the world that starts off the first time — and they shove away for the dock. Rod had asked me to put him on the dock before we anchored, thus saving him the trouble of getting in and out of the dinghy, above all of helping with the anchor. I acted as if I didn't hear him.

He bounds to the dock and goes leaping along toward the telephone booth. On the boat he is a great leaner and loller, very thoughtful in his movements, but ashore he is a gazelle.

"Monday night," I shout as he is about to disappear into the telephone booth.

"Keep a light burning," he shouts back.

The Man with the Big Gold Watch

2

A patch of hazy sunlight lies on the bay off to the south, but rivers of mist flow in through Golden Gate, following the streets as if they were riverbanks. The mist flows down the streets and into the heart of the city and eddies around the tall buildings so that only their tops show, like islands in a gray sea.

160

I remember the first time I came to San Francisco. I had just published my first book and arrived to give a small speech and to autograph copies of my book. There was an ad in the newspaper about the event, which at least thirty-two people must have read because thirty-two came to the autograph party.

The party was held in the back of a bookstore, in a room where cartons were usually stored. The cartons, or most of them, had been taken out and about fifty folding chairs set up in their places. There was a table against the wall with a hundred copies of my book piled on it, a picture of myself, the name of the book and my name under the picture.

The owner of the bookstore seated thirty people, scattering them around the room to make the crowd look larger than it was. Then he waited ten minutes past the time when I was to give my speech, hoping, I guess, that a few people might see the sign in the window and wander in. People stop to watch holes being dug in the ground or concrete being poured or steel girders being lifted, why shouldn't they stop and listen to an author speak?

Two more customers did wander in from the street. The bookman introduced me and I set off on my speech. There is nothing worse than an author's speech, especially the author of a first book. A plumber talking about the merits and demerits of a gooseneck fitting to the local chapter of the Pipefitters' Union is in comparison Philip addressing the Macedonians.

A man down in the front row, about five feet away from me as I spoke, kept looking at his watch. It was a big watch with a gold case that made a sharp click when he opened it and a sharp click when it was closed. He was one of the last two who had come wandering in from the street, so I figured that he had come in to put in the time while he was waiting for a bus or something. Anyway, the clicking of the big gold timepiece finally wore me down and with a dry throat and a stiff bow I ended my talk.

People gathered around the table, looked at my picture, then at me, picked up books, read a page here and there, then departed. All left except a handful, several of whom bought books and asked for my autograph. The last one to leave was the man who owned the big, noisy gold watch. He was of much less than average height, with kind eyes and a gentle face, a small man dressed in a neat brown suit.

He looked at the pile of books still lying on the table — eighty-five of them in their fresh, tomato-colored jackets.

"Do you like San Francisco?" he asked.

"Yes," I said, though at the moment, aware of the pile of unsold books, I was being less than truthful. "It's a beautiful city."

"I have always thought so, too," he said.

"But they don't buy books in San Francisco," I said, to ease my author's pride.

"Fifteen books isn't bad," the little man said. "I've been to autograph parties where only one or two books were sold."

I began to wonder about the man with the big gold watch, who had wandered in off the street, sat down, and quite obviously had heard nothing that I said. Did he make a habit of this sort of thing? Was he some kind of literary nut?

"Do you go to many autograph parties?" I asked, looking around for the owner of the store, as I edged out of the room with my hat in hand.

"All that I can, maybe one a week as an average."

A literary nut, all right. I said to myself.

The man walked over to the table and picked up one of the books from the pile and opened it. I paused in flight, thinking that he might have decided to ask for my autograph. I even took out my pen with a sort of flourish, hoping by the gesture to promote a sale.

The man put down the book and came over to where I was standing.

"Would you mind," he said, "if I asked you to put your name in all of the books? I know it's a big job, but I certainly would appreciate it."

I glanced around again for the owner of the bookstore, in mild terror seeking his help, sure now that I had encountered something that I could not cope with. The owner came, came running, as I remember, and introduced me to the man who wanted me to autograph all of the books.

His name was Albert Bender. And he did buy eighty-five books and I autographed them all and he had them sent out to schools and hospitals and prisons and old people's homes throughout the city and the countryside.

Albert Bender was rich, one of the rich men in San Francisco. If there was a writer or a painter or a sculptor or an artist of any kind who needed help, this dear and generous man helped him. San Francisco is called a great city. And it is great. Not because of its location between the sea and the Sierras, its magnificent harbor and its storybook past, but because of people like Albert Bender. San Francisco has had many people like him, men and women.

Gold! Gold!

3

John Sutter was not a San Franciscan. Yet like Bender he gave life to the city. This is how he did it.

Sutter was raised in Switzerland, failed as the owner of a bookstore, wisely sent his family to live with relatives, and headed for America in the hope of better luck. He traded on the Santa Fe Trail and in the Sandwich Islands, as Hawaii was then called. He showed up in California with a band of Sandwich Islanders and a boatload of trading goods. In the fall of 1839 he was on the American River with his band of dusky islanders, busy putting together a couple of big grass huts like the ones he had seen in Hawaii.

He built up a herd of cattle, though Indians and bandits preyed upon it regularly. Hearty and openhanded, he charmed the Mexicans into giving him a handsome grant of land. With the help of his islanders and some friendly Indians he planted fruit trees, set out wine grapes, and over the years built himself a fabled house which he called a fort, Sutter's Fort. It was like the castles he had admired in Switzerland and like the Mexican ranch houses that surrounded his land. Heavy adobe walls, some of them three feet thick, winding stairs, bastions, a courtyard in the shape of a hollow square, ringed around with all manner of shops, storerooms, bins, and vats.

Sutter needed lumber and flour so he sent one of his best workmen, James Marshall, up the American River to put together a saw and grist mill. While building the mill, Marshall built a tailrace. During the night he let water from the river flow through the race, but during the day he shut it off.

Early one morning — this was on the twenty-fourth of January in 1848 — he went down to the tailrace and shut off the water as was his custom.

"There, upon the rock," Marshall wrote in his memoirs, "about six inches beneath the surface of the water, I discovered gold.

" . . . I picked up one or two pieces and examined them attentively, and having some general knowledge of minerals, I could not call to mind more than two which in any way resembled this — sulphuret of iron, very bright and brittle; and gold, bright yet malleable."

If the piece of metal broke when it was pounded, it was sulfuret of iron and valueless. If it did not break, if instead it flattened out and held together, it was gold.

"I then tried it between two rocks," Marshall wrote, "and found that it could be beaten into a different shape, but not broken."

Four days later James Marshall went to the fort for provisions. He took along several pieces of the gold he had found in the tailrace. He was a silent man, secretive and dark-visaged with deep-set eyes that sometimes had a fanatic look about them.

Sutter wrote in his diary a description of their meeting:

"It was a rainy afternoon when Marshall arrived at my office at the fort. He was very wet, and I was surprised to see him, as he had been down a few days before. He told me he had some important business and interesting news, that he wanted to go to a place where we wouldn't be disturbed, where no one could listen, so I took him to my private rooms. He asked me to lock the door, and I did, though there was no one to fear as my desk clerk was busy in another room.

"Marshall asked me for something, so I opened the door and sent an Indian for it. Afterwards I forgot to lock the door, so that it so happened that just as Mr. Marshall took a rag from his pocket and was showing me the gold the clerk opened the door and came in. Marshall put the gold, about two ounce of it, right back into his pocket. The clerk went out. Then we looked at the small pieces of gold.

"I proved it with aqua-fortis, likewise with other experiments, and read a long article in the Encyclopedia Americana on gold, after which I declared this pure gold. Marshall wanted me to start right back to Coloma with him, but I told him the next morning would be time enough.

"I took the news easy, like all other occurrences, good or bad, but thought a great deal during the night about the consequences which might follow such a discovery."

Sutter and Marshall tried their best to keep the find a

secret but the news leaked out. In May a man named Sam Brannan hustled out of the hills and sloshed through San Francisco's muddy streets, shaking a bottle of glittering dust over his head and bellowing at the top of his lungs, "Gold! Gold! Gold! from the American River."

Sam Brannan's shouts emptied San Francisco. Sailors left their ships, carpenters dropped their hammers, storekeepers boarded up their stores, newspapermen, who had scoffed at rumors of gold, flung down their pens. Everyone headed for Coloma, leaving San Francisco a ghost town.

As for Coloma, where Sutter's unfinished sawmill stood, it was clawed to pieces. Overnight, almost, thousands rushed there from every corner of the state. From the nearby town of San Jose, for instance, came the jailer and a bunch of prisoners. Every foot of earth in the valley around Coloma was staked out and claimed. The valley itself was lowered twenty feet and more, by miners sluicing away the earth to get at the hidden gold.

Three Frenchmen yanked up a tree stump and picked off five thousand dollars' worth of nuggets that clung to its roots.

Mr. Wilson found two thousand dollars in nuggets under his doorstep.

A man with a claim only four feet square took out twenty pounds of gold.

Another man sat down on a rock to rest and discovered that he was sitting on pure gold.

An ex-soldier was riding along a bank of the Mokelumne River, saw a glint in the grass, and carried home a nugget that weighed twenty-six pounds. It was sent to Washington and put on display there and soon after it was displayed in the city of New York.

This nugget found by a riverbank launched a hundred thousand young men on the road to California. They crowded all the ports along the Atlantic coast and waited for ships that would take them around Cape Horn, or to Panama, where they could hike across the Isthmus and ship north to the goldfields. They crowded the banks of the Mississippi and got ready to strike out across the plains by wagon and horseback.

In '49 these thousands surged west into California. They dug for gold in places called Volcano, Whiskey Flat, Murderer's Ravine, Hangtown, Muletown, and Rattlesnake Gulch. Their ships stacked up against the shore not far from where we are anchored, so many crowded together that the masts looked like a forest.

This was the start of the city whose tall buildings now rise above a gray sea of fog.

Ship's Log

4

June 12: In the night the fog has blown away before a steady land wind and the dawn is clear. The wind gauge stands at five knots. The weather station reports good weather for Bodega Bay and Fort Ross and farther north. Perfect weather to start for the Columbia, but we can't leave without Rod, so we change filters, both water and oil — just in case we get some lumpy seas around Cape

Mendocino. I've never been to the Cape. Captains tell me that it's the worst stretch on the coast south of the Columbia River and Gray's Harbor . . . The navigator goes ashore to do some shopping. She's a slow shopper so I don't go along. She likes to look at the stacks of fresh, shining vegetables and fruits. I think that she likes to look at them better than she likes to eat them. She says it fortifies and strengthens her, just to look at them. This would solve a lot of problems if people got strength from looking at food instead of eating it . . . While the navigator is gone we move over to the fuel dock and fill the water and diesel tanks. As nearly as I can figure, we have used about five gallons an hour on the trip. Good mileage. Del fishes the rest of the afternoon and catches two very odd-looking fish, long-toothed and blunt-bodied, which he throws back. In the sea it pays to be odd looking, but not on land . . . We check the batteries and everything in the engine room, unit by unit, so there won't be any foul-ups in the morning . . . Supper on deck and enjoy a balmy evening with the wind light, still steady from the east. A good omen for tomorrow. Also enjoy thick slices of liver smothered with onions. I didn't like liver when I was a boy. There were a lot of things I didn't like when I was a boy that I like now: peanut butter, avocados, olives, artichokes, spinach, lettuce, and liver, to name a few. I think of the prices the '49ers paid for restaurant food: an egg cost a dollar; a peeled potato, seventy-five cents; a small dish of baked beans, seventy-five cents — if "greased," one dollar and ten cents. Even more than today. At six bells we decide not to wait up for Rod and go to bed.

ELEVEN

Waiting for Rod

1

$\mathbf{A}$ FEW MINUTES after the ship's bell strikes two I hear the sound of an automobile pulling up to the dock. I look out the porthole and see a taxi move away. I put on my pants and shoes and my windbreaker that still has two buttons missing, expecting to hear a shout from Rod — he has a good one — while I am getting myself together, but all is silence.

When I go up on deck to start the motor in the dinghy there's a man standing on the dock under a light with a suitcase in his hand and his hat pulled down over his eyes. It is not Rod, so I go back to the cabin and lie down with my clothes on and wait for the next taxi. Two more taxis pull up before dawn and disembark passengers, but Rodney Lambert is not among them.

I go out on deck as the sun comes up and find Del sitting on the stern, fishing rod in hand.

"Nice day," I begin.

The bay is flat and streaked with dawn colors, dove gray and shades of pink and dark blue. The morning wind is light, still from the east.

Del has a bite on his line and takes his time in answering. "Sure is," he says when he decides that the fish is not going to bite again. "Yes, a mighty nice day."

"Have you seen anything of Rod?"

"No, and haven't heard from him either."

Del is referring to the fact that Rod snores a lot, loud and many-toned.

The navigator comes out with a plate of homemade sweet rolls and a pot of coffee. She looks fresh-faced, having slept soundly, unaware of the taxis that drove up to the dock throughout the night, or that Rod is not on board.

"Our wandering boy has not returned," I inform her. "What do you want to do?"

"We'll have to wait."

"How long?"

"I don't know. We can't just go off and leave him."

"Why not?" I ask.

"It wouldn't be right."

"What if he doesn't show up until tomorrow or the next day or until next week sometime?"

"If he doesn't come by this afternoon, then, well, let's leave."

"We can't leave this afternoon. If we're going we should go now before the wind builds up outside."

Del has another bite on his line. He pulls in a fish, one of the fat, long-toothed kind, and tosses it back.

"Whatever the two of you want to do," he says wisely. "It makes no difference to me except that I would like to find some place where the fishing is good."

Since we left Monterey we have never mentioned the letter the ship broker sent us. It was more than an unpleasant surprise, that warning against Lambert, it was a reflection somehow on our judgment in hiring someone we knew nothing about. It even made me want to prove the broker wrong. After a couple of sleepless nights, I have changed my mind.

"We can handle the boat ourselves," I say. "We don't need Rod. As a matter of fact, he's just in the way. We're lucky to be rid of him. We've gotten off easy, I would say, when you think of the damage he has done to other boats he's been around."

"I'll feel better if we wait until afternoon," the navigator says.

We drink a cup of coffee and eat a sweet roll. It is already late for a good start. But if Rod should happen along within an hour, we can get ready and go. We drink another cup of coffee and wait, keeping our eyes on the street that leads down to the dock.

"Did you pay Rod all his wages?" the navigator asks. "I paid him for last week but not for this week. He hasn't finished the week yet. And it doesn't look as if he plans to."

"He'll be along," Del says.

"When?" I ask.

"When his money runs out."

I climb up to the flydeck where I can get a better view of the shore. In about ten minutes a taxi drives up and a woman gets out with two dogs. I go back down and stand at the stern with the navigator and Del. We all have another cup of coffee and finish the sweet rolls, then go inside and watch the early news on TV. Every time I hear a car come down to the dock I get up and look out.

We wait all morning for Rod. We have lunch and wait all afternoon. We have supper and wait until eleven o' clock. Then everybody goes to bed and sleeps except me. I still expect Rod to come. Through the night, I hear noises of all sorts — cars, boats, outboards starting up, outboards not starting up, even the duck in the bilge prowling around.

I have just fallen asleep when the sound of footsteps, lights in the galley, and bacon frying wake me. I get myself dressed and go up to find breakfast on the table. The navigator has already laid out our course for the day and the chart with her figures stands in front of the wheel.

No one mentions Rodney Lambert.

I start the engine and let it warm up while we eat. We bring in the anchor, take one last look toward the dock, and head west toward Golden Gate Bridge. The bridge spans one mile of the bay in one giant leap, stands more than two hundred feet above the water, is held aloft by three million feet of cable larger than your wrist, and yet it seems to float beyond us in the air, fairylike in the strong morning light.

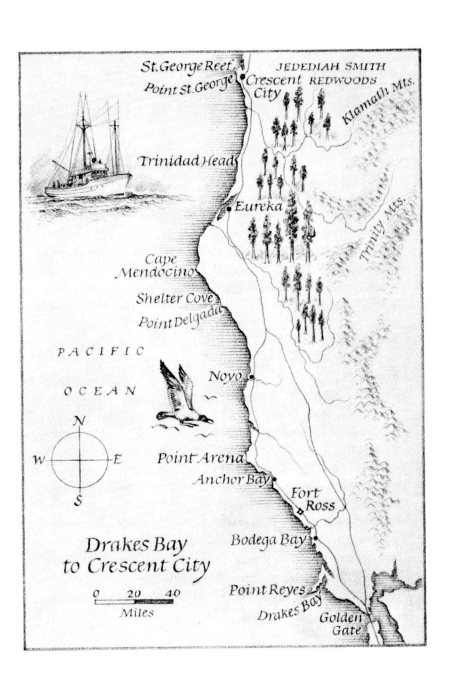

St. George Reef

Point St. George

Crescent City

JEDEDIAH SMITH

REDWOODS

Klamath Mts.

Trinidad Heads

Eureka

Trinity Mts.

Cape Mendocino

Shelter Cove

Point Delgada

PACIFIC

OCEAN

Noyo

N

W · E

S

Point Arena

Anchor Bay

Fort Ross

Bodega Bay

Drakes Bay
to Crescent City

0   20   40
Miles

Point Reyes

Drakes Bay

Golden Gate

Gentleman Pirate

2

We travel a few miles beyond the Gate and turn right. The long Pacific swells lift us slowly and let us down, but they are friendly and well-spaced and their surface is like marble. Off to port are the windy Farallones, to starboard the Marin shore, not far away to the north lies the cove where Sir Francis Drake once found shelter from the Arctic cold.

Sir Francis never went to school. Instead he went to sea and by the time he was twenty-four commanded his first ship. Ten years later, in 1577, he sailed off from England on a voyage around the world.

A company of adventurers gave him the money to outfit his ships. Queen Elizabeth gave him her royal blessing. The company and the queen hoped that he would open a profitable spice trade between England and the Orient. If possible, to find the Straits of Anian, which many thought joined the Atlantic and Pacific Oceans somewhere to the north of California. Drake himself was less ambitious. His chief desire was to rummage around on the Pacific Coast and gather up all the loot he could lay his hands upon.

He had a fleet of four small ships and a pinnace. His crew was made up of English and French and Scots, a sprinkling from all over, including a few blacks. The flagship of the fleet was the *Pelican* — later renamed *Golden Hind.* She was only twenty feet longer than the

Arctic Star, but she had a crew of some ninety men, fourteen cannon, twelve of them cast iron and two of them brass, and a quantity of small arms. A crowded little ship for a trip around the world!

While still in the Atlantic Drake decided to lighten his fleet, and thus make it easier to handle, by burning two of the ships. With the three that were left he rounded the Horn, but before he had traveled far along the coast of South America storms wrecked one of the ships and frightened the captain of another so badly that he left Drake and sailed back to England.

Drake cruised on, up the coast of Chile, seizing Spanish cargoes right and left, swearing that he would not stop until he had taken goods to the value of several million English pounds, a sum that the Spaniards had stolen from his pirate cousin, John Hawkins. Yet he was always courteous to his victims. Sometimes he even invited them to dinner on board the *Golden Hind*, serving them at tables set with fine linen and silver, while his own private orchestra performed for their pleasure and astonishment.

Drake worked his way northward past Panama and Acapulco. He looted whenever he could, scared the Spaniards half to death, and finally, when the *Golden Hind* was in bad shape, put into the bay we are now approaching. His diarist wrote an account of his stay, portions of which follow, changed from Elizabethan into modern English.

"The fifth day of June [1579], being in 43° toward the pole Arctic, we found the air so cold that our men, being grievously pinched with the same, complained of the extremity thereof, and the farther we went the more cold

176

increased upon us. Whereupon we thought it best for that time to seek the land, and did so, finding it not mountainous, but low plain land, and clad and covered over with snow, so that we drew back again without landing till we came within 38° toward the line, in which height it pleased God to send us into a fair and good bay with a good wind to enter the same.

"In this bay we anchored, and the people of the country, having their houses close by the water's side, showed themselves unto us, and sent a present to our general. When they came unto us, they greatly wondered at the things that we brought, but our general, according to his natural and accustomed humanity, courteously treated them and liberally bestowed on them necessary things to cover their nakedness, whereupon they supposed us to be gods and would not be persuaded to the contrary.

" . . . The news of our being there, being spread through the country, the people that inhabited round about came down, and amongst them the king [chief] himself.

" . . . In the forefront was a man of goodly personage who bore the scepter or mace before the king, whereupon hung two crowns, a less and a bigger, with three chains of a marvelous length.

" . . . Next unto him which bore the scepter was the king himself, with his guard about his person, clad with cony skins and other skins . . .

"They made signs to our general to sit down, to whom the king and divers others made several orations, or rather supplications, that he would take their province and king-dom into his hand and become their king, making signs that they would resign unto him their right and title to the whole land and become his subjects.

"In which to persuade us the better, the king and the rest, with one consent and with great reverence, joyfully singing a song, did set the crown upon his head, enriched his neck with all their chains and offered unto him many other things.

" . . . Wherefore in the name and to the use of her Majesty, he took the scepter, crown and dignity of the said country into his hands . . .

"The common sort of people, leaving the king and his guard with our general, scattered themselves, together with their sacrifices, among our people, taking a diligent view of every person; and such as pleased their fancy, which were the youngest, they enclosing them about, offered their sacrifices unto them with lamentable weeping, scratching and tearing the flesh from their faces with their nails, whereof issued abundance of blood.

"But we used signs to them of disliking this and stayed their hands from force, and directed them upward to the living God, whom only they ought to worship . . ."

The Indians Drake met and whose king he became held the belief that a white god would someday come to rule over them — a belief they shared with the Aztecs, whom they had never seen or heard of. Drake's treatment of them is also interesting. Patiently he bore their sacrifices and humility and, tough as he was, he even was touched, in contrast to many of the Spanish conquistadores — Guzman, for instance, who tied the chief of the Tarascan Indians to the tail of a horse, had him dragged around the town square, and then tossed into a bonfire.

Ship's Log

3

June 14: As we leave Drakes Bay and round Point Reyes, which is shaped like a big fishhook, we encounter a freshening wind. The wind builds and by noon the sea is kicking up its heels. We change our plans of making Anchor Bay by dark and decide to spend the night at Bodega Bay. We pass two ships close to starboard heading south, both of them in ballast and making sloppy weather of it, even though they are traveling with the wind. We make Bodega Bay at an early hour, which gives Del a chance to catch fish for supper. They should taste good after three fishless days.

June 15: Thin fog out of Bodega but it burns off by midmorning, leaving us blue skies and far horizons. Off at some distance we sight a great gathering of waterfowl. Thousands. Dipping and darting, milling around a common center that proves to be, as we come nearer, an enormous school of anchovies. The fowl that have gorged themselves are floating around on the edge of the school, too heavy to fly, stretching their necks in an effort to stretch their stomachs and make room for more anchovies. The din is deafening. We recognize a Heermann's Gull, which is now rare along the coast, a beautiful slate-colored bird with a white head. Hundreds of Sooty Shearwaters that breed around Cape Horn and fly northward for the summer. Hundreds of Bonaparte's Gulls, the daintiest of all the gulls. Hundreds of Tufted Puffins. These birds nest in burrows lined with feathers and grass along the rocky headlands of California and Oregon, laying one spotted egg at a time. They are often called Sea Parrots and for good reason. They have big, bright -colored beaks, dark at the tips, and bright red farther along, white on their faces, and a long crest of yellow feathers over each eye. Their wings are small and blunt, which makes it difficult for them to rise from the sea on a windless day. But once in the air they fly like bullets. In his white face and yellow plumes and his big red beak, like a false nose, he looks as if he might be on his way to a masquerade . . . We reach Anchor Bay after a six-hour run. A beautiful bay, though open to the west. We are sneaking up on Cape Mendocino. One step at a time, one harbor at a time. We are trying to be in a position from which we can make an early start and pass the Cape before the wind starts to blow. There is always a heavy swell at Cape Mendocino, but we would like to avoid the combination of swell and wind that adds up to rough water.

Voice in the Night

4

We are anchored close to the beach in about four fathoms, just outside the breaker line, on a good-holding sandy bottom. The afternoon wind has died down and we are getting a breeze that seems to be wandering around in the bay from one shore to the other. Del is on the stern with his fishing rod — we should rig up a bunk for him there so that he could fish while he sleeps. He is casting toward the shore, long casts that fall just short of the breakers, a spot where he should pick up a surf fish or two. The navigator and I are reading and have the ship-to-shore turned on for the eight o'clock weather report.

The report is for fair weather and the usual afternoon winds from fifteen to twenty knots. I get up and walk over to the radio-telephone and have my hand on the knob to turn it off when a voice, a familiar voice, stops my hand. I look at the navigator. She has heard what I have heard and she is looking at me. I turn up the volume and get a sharper tuning.

"It sounds like David Brinkley," the navigator says.

"What's Brinkley doing out here?"

The navigator comes over to where I am standing. We both listen.

"It sounds like somebody else, too," she says.

"It sounds a little like Rodney Lambert," I say. "He's always giving imitations--Cary Grant, W. C. Fields, Nixon, somebody. He could be giving an imitation of Brinkley."

"What would Rod be doing out here giving an imitation of Brinkley?"

"Rod doesn't have a voice of his own, you know."

The voice is talking to someone who gives his position as twenty miles south of Anchor Bay. In return the voice gives its position as the Golden Gate.

The words come out very clear, though we are near the receiving limit of our set. Clear and clipped, a little like Brinkley's, deep-toned and slow and bored.

The voice that is coming from twenty miles away signs off. It is the skipper of the *Betsy Lou* bound for Astoria. Then, still clear and clipped and bored, the other voice answers:

"This is Captain Rodney Lambert of the *Island Eagle*. Good night, *Betsy Lou*, see you in Astoria."

We look at each other with our mouths open. But before either of us can speak we hear Rod Lambert's voice again, coming to us from San Francisco.

"*Island Eagle* calling *Arctic Star*. *Island Eagle* calling *Arctic Star* . . ."

The call goes on while we stand there speechless.

"Captain Rodney Lambert calling Captain Mizrael. Captain Lambert calling Captain Mizrael of the *Arctic Star*. Captain Mizrael . . ."

"Who is Mizrael?" I ask the navigator.

"You know," she says, "he's the archangel who sees that inferiors obey their superiors. He's one of the seventy-two angels bearing the name of God Shemhamphorae."

"He is?" I answered lamely. "Is that so?"

Rodney has a new name for me now. At least it sounds better than Ratso. Or does it?

The voice goes on, "*Island Eagle* calling *Arctic Star*. . ."

"You had better answer," the navigator says.

"Why?"

"If you don't, he'll pester the life out of us."

I pick up the receiver and flip the switch on the handle. "*Arctic Star. Arctic Star.* We hear you, *Island Eagle*. Over."

I touch the switch and listen.

"Hi there. How are you? How's the Missus? How's Del? Has he bumped his head on the engine-room beam again?"

"Everyone's fine and how are you?"

"Fine."

"We missed you in Sausalito."

"Yeah. I phoned a couple of times but couldn't get through."

"That's too bad."

Is it possible that he has hitched a ride and is trying to catch up with us? Does he want us to anchor somewhere along the coast and wait for him? The thought sends a chill through me, through the cabin.

"Who is your new boss?" I ask quickly, thinking to head off any such idea.

"John Hannah," Rod answers. "He owns ten stores in Frisco. He's a millionaire."

"He needs to be," I can't help saying.

I turn the phone over to Rod, relieved that he has a new job, in my thoughts wishing him well, also wishing Mr. Hannah well, and the *Island Eagle* especially well.

I wait. I can hear Rod breathing. I can almost hear him thinking.

"Pardon the delay," he says. "I had to adjust the set. It's more sensitive than the one on the *Arctic Star* . . . has a range of three hundred miles."

Three hundred miles is twice our range.

"I was wondering," he goes on, "if you could send the money you owe me to Eureka? General Delivery, Eureka. I'll pick it up there in four days. You can mail it from

Noyo. It would be better if you wired it."

Rod is still talking in his David Brinkley voice, slow and clear and loud, so loud that the navigator has no trouble hearing him.

I shut off the phone and we confer for a moment.

"I'll mail the money from Noyo," I tell Rod.

"Thanks, man. That'll be great," he says. "Thanks a lot, man. I'll call you tomorrow, same time. Good night, all. Captain Lambert aboard the *Island Eagle* signing off. Over."

"Good night," I say, and shut down the set, pleased, nay, delighted at the way things have turned out.

TWELVE

Ship's Log

1

June 16: A dawn departure in the hope of outwitting the westerlies. Fine cruising until we pass Point Arena and meet steady headwinds. We slow down to six knots to ease the rollicking motion, then to five knots. Rivers empty into the sea along here, and from here northward logs, stumps, and branches wash down from the forests. It is wise to keep on the lookout for debris that can stove a hole in the hull or snap a propeller. Most of it you see, but once in a while you can stumble upon a deadhead, a log floating on end, just the end showing but with thirty feet of timber underneath. We have passed Fort Ross — country the Russians settled in the early 1800's — and reach Noyo in time to send Rod a check by afternoon mail. Noyo is a fishing center with a small protected harbor lively with boats and canneries and fish smells. During supper we hear Rod on the radio telephone, but don't interrupt him.

He's chinning with someone in San Francisco.

June 17: An early start for Shelter Cove and we arrive before the seas build up. The chart shows rocks and shoals to seaward and we pick our way carefully, using the depth finder. Once inside we are well protected except from the southwest, since the cove lies in the lee of Point Delgada. We call the Coast Guard to get the weather forecast for Cape Mendocino, but before we can hang up Rod greets us from the *Island Eagle*. He wants to know if we have sent his wages to Eureka. He will be there in two days. *Island Eagle* cruises at twelve knots, he says, which is two knots faster than we can go. He expects to pass us between Eureka and the Columbia River. If he does pass us, I hope that it is during the night, a dark night. He signs off wishing us a good trip around Mendocino, calling me Captain Barattiel this time. Barattiel, the navigator informs me, is the angelic prince with three fingers with which he is able to hold up the heavens. There is nothing like a talk with Rod Lambert to spoil an evening. I try listening to the radio. I try to read. Finally I go out on the stern. The cannery smells have abated. There's a fresh wind coming down from the mountains and the forests. The night is clear. Overhead and to the west there's a small smudge in the sky. It is no larger to the eye than the print of your thumb. It is Hercules 13, a galaxy of one hundred thousand suns, all of them larger than our sun. Thinking about Hercules 13, I forget Rod Lambert.

June 18: A red-sky-in-the-morning-sailors-take-warning kind of day with smoke-colored clouds to the north

186

and an orange-streaked sky in the east. But the Coast Guard forecast, which has promised fair weather, turns out to be right. The wind and sea are moderate as we round Cape Mendocino late in the morning, as moderate as you are apt to find along this stormy coast. After days of expecting the worst, we are almost disappointed with the weather. We were ready to meet a lion and instead we meet a mouse. But our disappointment doesn't last very long. We are still at sea where anything can happen . . . a rugged and beautiful shore to starboard, a towering surf and black cliffs and blue mountains beyond. A school of dolphins comes from somewhere astern. *Arctic Star* is going along at a good clip but they have no trouble overtaking it. They gather to greet us, just ahead of our plunging prow, sometimes touching it. They weave back and forth in intricate foamy patterns, their undersides flashing white. The sound of their breathing is like the rustle of silk. They enjoy people, these beautiful mammals. They enjoy tuna also and the tuna enjoy them. They often travel the world's seas in great schools together. That is why some three hundred thousand dolphins die every year, entangled in the tuna nets. The tuna fishermen could catch tuna and not catch dolphins by devising nets with smaller mesh. But so far they haven't gotten around to it. * Two hours later we reach the river bar at Eureka. The navigator has timed our arrival to meet the flooding tide. With the wind northwest and the wrong tide, this entrance is dangerous. We dock in the lower part of the harbor and, while the navigator goes shopping, Del and I tinker in the engine room, inspecting

*Tuna fishing standards designed to protect dolphins have improved considerably since the first publication of this book.

the filters, topping the batteries, checking everything for our voyage up the Oregon coast . . . The noon weather report is favorable so we plan to leave in the morning for Crescent City. Trinidad Head lies only two hours along the way, and if the weather worsens we will put in there. On this coast it pays to have a secondary harbor in mind, even a third harbor — places you can duck into in case of a sudden storm.

Wrecks

2

From Cape Mendocino to the Columbia River and north to Destruction Island and Cape Flattery, the coast is hazardous. In this stretch of waters more than three thousand ships have been sunk, more than one hundred and fifty at Cape Flattery, almost two thousand ships around the Columbia River bar alone, where more than fifteen hundred lives have been lost.

After we leave Crescent City in the morning we pass St. George Reef. This reef extends for six and one half miles northwest of Point St. George. Here on a summer day the *Brother Jonathan* went aground. The ship's quartermaster, who was on duty at the time, describes the disaster:

"I took the wheel at twelve o'clock. A northwest gale was blowing and we were four miles above St. George. The sea was running mountain high and the ship was not making headway. The captain thought it best to turn back to Crescent City and wait until the storm had ceased.

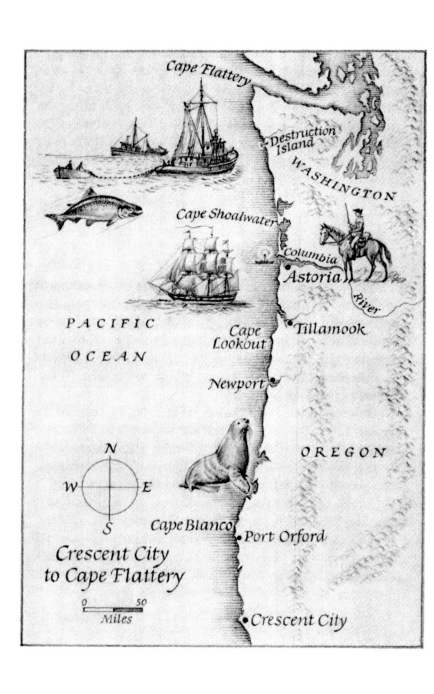

Cape Flattery

Destruction
Island

WASHINGTON

Cape Shoalwater

Columbia

Astoria

River

PACIFIC

OCEAN

Cape
Lookout

Tillamook

Newport

N

W   E

S

OREGON

Cape Blanco

Port Orford

Crescent City
to Cape Flattery

0   50
Miles

Crescent City

He ordered the helm hard aport. I obeyed and it steadied her. I kept due east. This was about 12:45. When we made Seal Rock the captain said, 'Southeast by south.' It was clear where we were, but foggy and smokey inshore. We ran till 1:50 when she struck with great force, knocking the passengers down and starting the deck planks. The captain stopped and backed her, but could not move the vessel an inch. She rolled about five minutes, then gave a tremendous thump and part of the keel came up alongside. By that time the wind and sea had slewed her around until her head came to the sea and she worked off a little. Then the foremast went through the bottom until the yard rested on the deck. Captain De Wolf ordered everyone to look to his own safety and said that he would do the best he could for all."

The ship was swept from the reef and quickly sank, taking with her one hundred and sixty-six passengers and crew. She also took to the bottom an Army payroll worth more than two hundred and fifty thousand dollars, which never has been found.

We give St. George Reef a wide berth.

Ship's Log Continued

3

June 20: We pass the redwoods named in honor of Jed Smith. They stand along the Smith River in the Six Rivers country, about twelve miles from the coast, just above Point St. George, and barely visible on a ridge. Jed would be proud of this tribute. He liked trees and running rivers.

Reach Port Orford late in the afternoon after a good cruise along the shore, zigzagging in and out among boats trolling for salmon. Del has had a line out but with no luck, though lots of fish are being caught. We travel too fast for salmon, which don't like to chase after the bait. It is a choice between catching fish and getting to the harbor during daylight. A strange harbor, one you have never seen before, can be treacherous after dark.

A small anchorage but well protected from the northwest by Cape Blanco, surrounded on three sides by hills and mountains covered with Port Orford cedar. These giant evergreens furnish the best of all the woods for the planking of small boats. Soft yellow in color, unattractive to marine borers and pests, long-fibered, sweet-smelling and tough, it lasts a lifetime and longer. It is the same variety as Alaskan cedar, with which *Artic Star* is planked. The supply is very short, due to over cutting.

Del scouts around through the harbor and comes back with a six-pound salmon, costing one dollar. A good bargain and, since there's nothing better than fresh-broiled salmon, we have a fine feast.

Our next call before the Columbia River is Newport. Weather rumors continue favorable . . . Hear Rod on the telephone, talking to a marine mechanic in Eureka. He is in Crescent City for some sort of minor repairs. He calls the *Arctic Star* but we are all too tired to talk, so don't answer. He has made fast time in heavy seas and his trouble is likely due to speed.

Red Sky in the Morning

4

The weather holds fair to Newport, but as we leave at dawn for the Columbia River the sky is streaked with thin orange streamers that seem to burst like a rocket out of the east. By noon the wind is heavy and we decide to put in at Tillamook for the night rather than buck the wind all afternoon and then make the Columbia bar too late for the tide.

We leave early from Tillamook but take our time, trolling for salmon at a speed of three knots. There's a multitude of boats fishing — I count ninety-two in less than an hour — with their long poles out and their lines trailing far astern. Most of them are trolling north and south on a course parallel to ours. But now and then we come upon a boat that is trolling east and west, crosswise to us, and we have to slow down or stop to let him pass, which can be annoying.

Toward noon, as the surface of the sea begins to form small white caps, I notice that many of the fishermen have drawn in their lines and are heading for shelter. Though the wind has not risen much, we take the hint and make for the Columbia at full speed. We hope to arrive there about an hour after flood tide, a good time to cross the bar.

About three o'clock in the afternoon we sight a boat coming upon our stern. She turns out to be the *Island*

Eagle. She is sleek and white and looks to be a sixty-footer.

As she comes abreast of us, I see that Captain Rod Lambert is at the wheel. He opens a window and gives us a sweeping wave and at the same time two blasts on his air horn. I give him two blasts in return and off he goes, leaving us astern, with a big wake to wallow in for a while.

The wind has died to about five knots but now the sky has an odd look, as if it had been smeared with skimmed milk.

Weather is strange and, for various reasons, never the same for long. More than five million billion tons of air are squeezed down hard against the earth. The sun warms this ocean of air. The night cools it. Big winds form over smooth surfaces and are deflected by the spinning of the earth upon its axis. The South and North Poles breed winds. So do the tropics. Winds may start in one place and end up two thousand miles away. There is always something going on in this big ocean of air.

It is about four o'clock when the wind hits us. Most of the fishing boats have found cover in dog holes along the coast. Since noon the swells have been normal for this area. They have borne down all day out of the Aleutians, round-shouldered and gray, about thirty feet high from valley to crest, traveling at about thirty knots. The wind that begins to gust at forty miles an hour doesn't change the size or the rhythm of the swells. They come on regularly, as they have all morning and the early afternoon, still thirty feet high and traveling at thirty knots. But on their backs the wind now builds up thousands of pinnacles and tumbling peaks.

There is nothing for us to do except to run and take it, to slow down when the wind gusts and speed up when it eases off. The boat puts her nose under and lifts green water that sluices down the decks and pours through the scuppers. The forward deck is covered with a cloud of spray. She is as uncomfortable as a bucking mule.

Our trouble now is that we will not reach the Columbia at the right time. Even if the storm doesn't get worse, we will be there a half an hour too late for the end of the flood tide. There is nothing to do about this but to take things as they come and to hope that the storm has reached its peak.

Through spray and drifting mist we sight the lightship anchored off the river bar. Beside her, like chicks around a mother hen, are three fishing boats. They are bobbing about in the lee of the big, iron-hulled ship, moving forward and astern but trying to keep the lightship between them and the wind.

The radio telephone is on and we hear the Coast Guard talking to the skipper of one of the boats in the lee of the lightship. He has been out for five days and has a load of salmon, which is going to spoil because his ice machine has broken down.

Between us and the bar, at a distance of a quarter mile, I make out the *Island Eagle*. Apparently she has been inshore to take a look at the river entrance and is coming back. Then we hear Captain Rod Lambert talking to the lightship.

"It's better inside than out here," he tells the lightship operator.

"It only looks that way," the operator replies.

A moment or two later Rod is talking to the Coast Guard. They don't talk long. The Coast Guard advises him to stay away from the entrance and the river.

Then I hear Rod calling the *Arctic Star* and I answer. He calls me by my right name. The storm must have sobered him.

"I got into one off Gray's Harbor two years ago, worse than this," he says. "What's up with you?"

"We're making rough weather, I answer, but we'll stick it out."

"For six hours, man?"

I can see the *Island Eagle* from where I stand at the wheel. She is throttled down and circling, rolling from beam-end to beam-end. But she looks seaworthy. She's a pretty ship, with a sweeping, graceful sheer and two bright flags flying.

"We've got plenty of power," Rod says. "Four hundred horses. Man, we can climb a wall."

"That's what you'll have to do if you go in," I say.

Another skipper comes on, calling the lightship, and when he finishes Rod has signed off. I have my hands full trying to keep the bow into the wind, at the same time to stay clear of the other boats, so I don't see the *Island Eagle* leave. Del says that she is heading for the entrance.

"You don't suppose he will try to make it," the navigator says.

"He might," Del says. "He's just wild enough and cocky enough."

"Won't the Coast Guard do something?" the navigator asks.

"Do what?" I answer.

"Warn him."

"They have done that already. But that's all they can do. They can't stop him."

"Maybe he can make it," Del says. "Those four hundred horses just might get him through."

"Also he might change his mind," I say. "Once he gets a close look at the bar he may back off and wait for the tide."

The bar is very dangerous now. The river flows at a steady rate, but it is a big river. Against it at this moment, while the tide is flooding, crash the powerful Pacific swells — the gray, hump-backed swells that are thirty feet high and move along at thirty knots. The sea tries to crash into the river mouth. In turn the river tries to push back the sea. The two great forces meet head on. Their meeting creates a maelstrom of conflicting water. The water is torn apart, revealing the sand beneath. It mounts into hills. It is sucked away into valleys. It grinds and lashes violently in one direction, then in another, then in all directions. That is why over the years almost two thousand ships have been destroyed at the Columbia River bar.

The wind blows from the northwest, high-pitched and insistent, like a hungry dog whining at the door. The lightship is not much of a shelter for her bobbing brood. She is having a rough time of it herself, pitching and rolling and taking great dollops of green water aboard. But just her presence, just her being there between us and the throat of the wind, is a comfort.

Strangely, through all the tumult of wind and waves, a flock of phalaropes attend us. They fly past, low over the sea, its heaving hills and deep valleys. They disappear in the spray and wheel back, then light nearby. These beautiful little birds are no more than puffs of dusky feathers and yet they are the most seaworthy things around, riding high and free in defiance of the storm.

At six o'clock the wind slackens, at least I can hear it no longer. At seven exactly — I know the time because the ship's clock strikes the hour — we hear two Coast Guard vessels talking. One is at Astoria, a few miles up the river, and the other near the north jetty. At first I think that they are talking to each other. Then there's an explosion of static, followed by a moment of silence. I make out that the two vessels are talking to the pilot of a Coast Guard plane that is flying back and forth at the mouth of the river.

A voice that we all recognize breaks in. The first of the words are blurred. It is Rod Lambert giving the position of the *Island Eagle*. She is a half-mile off the south jetty, moving toward the river mouth.

There's a short period of quiet, more static, then the two Coast Guard vessels are talking at once, followed in a moment by Rod's voice. He is shouting the three call letters of a ship in distress. He repeats the call. It is the first time I have ever heard his real voice. I guess it is his real voice because this time it doesn't sound like anyone else's voice.

He calls again, but only two of the three call letters of a ship in distress.

We wait for them to talk again. After a few minutes of silence we turn on the radio. We know, of course, that the Coast Guard is hurrying toward the *Island Eagle*.

I wonder if they are thinking of the day just a few years ago when three of their vessels were sunk trying to rescue a fishing boat.

There is nothing that we can do to help, except to keep out of the way and not get into trouble ourselves. Our hands are full with the *Arctic Star*, but we keep listening to the radio and the ship-to-shore.

About eight, on a broadcast from Portland, which is up the river from us, we get the first news of the *Island Eagle*. She has been torn apart and scattered against the north jetty. The captain of the ship, Rodney Lambert of San Diego, has saved Mr. and Mrs. John Hannah and two children from death by an astonishing act of bravery. On further broadcasts that evening we get the details of Rod Lambert's heroism. (The next morning there's a picture of him in the newspaper, smiling and looking handsomely heroic in a torn shirt.)

By midnight the storm has blown itself out. When the tide floods and is about to ebb we leave the lightship, cross the bar and go into the river, traveling along behind the fishing boats who know the way. There are a few stars in the sky now and they cast their reflections on the river.

We follow the fishermen to the fishing harbor in Astoria. We find a berth, although the harbor is crowded.

Our voyage to the Columbia is over. Del has caught a lot of fish, if not the big one. The big one still swims the ocean deeps and he can dream about it on long winter nights, which may be more satisfying than if he had caught it. The navigator has tested her skills against wind and wave and the quirks of chart and compass. Rod Lambert

— I am certain nothing could please him more — has become an instant hero, at least to some. The *Arctic Star* has behaved well and we are proud of her. In the morning, in appreciation, we will go through her carefully. With good fortune we may find the quacking duck that lurks somewhere in the bilge. As for me, I have admired since my childhood the young captains who once sailed our western shores, many in leaky ships, some without charts, even the comfort of a single buoy or one lonely lighthouse. Now that I have traveled in their wakes, my admiration for them and their durable crews is boundless.

More stars come out. A small piece of moon shows among the trailing clouds. We are moored near the channel and I can hear salmon leaping. They have come from the open sea on their way to the headwaters of the Columbia, to the streams and rivulets where they were born.

INDEX

San Pasqual, Battle of, 20, 22-32, 147
San Pedro, 58, 65, 68, 81, 84, 89, 98, 103, 115, 144
San Salvador (caravel), 7, 108
Sand, creation of, 18
Santa Barbara, 114-117, 120, 144, 149
Santa Barbara Channel (the Canal), 105, 125-127, 129
Santa Catalina Island, 103
Santa Rosa (frigate), 145
Santa Rosa Island, 104, 109
Sardines, 44, 155
Scammons Lagoon, 43

Scripps Institute of Oceanography, 15, 43
Sea, sounds of the, 15-16
Sea otter, 44, 130-33, 135-38
Sea Parrot, 180
Sea World, 42-43
Serra, Father Junípero, xi, 12-14, 105, 140-43, 158
Sessions, Kate, 17-18
Shearwater, Sooty, 179
Smith, Jedediah, xi, 70-80, 189-90
Starvation Peak, 20, 22, 29-32, 147. *See also* San Pasqual, Battle of

Stevenson, Robert Louis, 146
Stockton, Commodore, 28-29, 32, 147-148, 153-154
Sutter, John, xi, 164-67
Swordfish, 33-42

Treasure Island, 146
Two Years before the Mast, 50, 51, 54-56, 58-63, 89

Vizcaíno, Sebastián, 10-11, 105-106, 109

Whales, 16, 43-45, 102

203

Suggested Reading

Between Pacific Tides, Edward Ricketts and Jack Calvin. (Stanford: Stanford University Press, 1968. Fourth edition.) A basic book about the seashore. Illustrated.

The California Feeling, Peter Beagle and Michael Bry. (New York: Doubleday, 1971.) Beagle does the writing and Bry the photography in this fine book about a tour in an old bus.

Edge of the Continent, Don Graeme Kelley. (Palo Alto: American West, 1971.) The Pacific Coast from Alaska to Mexico through the eyes of a perceptive naturalist. Many maps and handsome photographs.

A Field Guide to Western Birds, Roger Tory Peterson. (Boston: Houghton Mifflin, 1961. Second edition.) Handiest of the guides. Illustrated.

Glory, God and Gold, Paul I. Wellman. (New York: Doubleday, 1956.) Four hundred years in the turbulent history of the Southwest.

The House of Life, Paul Brooks. (Boston: Houghton Mifflin, 1972). Stories about the great naturalist, Rachel Carson, by her editor. Illustrated.

The Immense Journey, Loren Eiseley. (New York: Random House, 1957.) A classic by a poet-naturalist.

Island of the Blue Dolphins, Scott O'Dell. (Boston: Houghton Mifflin, 1960.) The true story of an Indian girl who lived on San Nicolas Island for eighteen years alone.

Men to Match My Mountains, Irving Stone. (New York: Doubleday, 1956.) A dramatic account of the West from 1540 to 1900.

A Natural History of Western Trees, edited by Donald Culross Peattie. (Boston: Houghton Mifflin, 1953.) A glowing guide by one of the best of the nature writers. Illustrated.

The Ocean of Air, David I. Blumenstock. (New Brunswick, N.J.: Rutgers University Press, 1959.) Startling facts about the air we live in.

The Royal Highway, Edwin Corle. (New York: Bobbs-Merrill, 1949.) Follows the path of the padres in California. Illustrated.

The Sea Around Us, Rachel Carson. (New York: Oxford University Press, 1961. Revised edition.) A beautiful and essential book. Illustrated.

Songs of the Humpback Whale. (Del Mar, California: CRM Records.) Mysterious voices from the ocean deeps recorded by scientists.

Westward Tilt: The American West Today, Neil Morgan. (New York: Random House, 1963.) As seen by the popular California columnist. Maps.

Where Have All the Flowers, Fishes, Birds, Trees, Water and Air Gone?, Osborn Segerberg, Jr. (New York: McKay, 1971.) Interesting answers.

The Year of the Whale, Victor B. Scheffer. (New York: Scribner, 1969.) An exciting odyssey of the world's largest mammal. Illustrated.

CPSIA information can be obtained at www.ICGtesting.com
Printed in the USA
BVOW05s1520030814

360960BV00001B/1/P